Ludwig van Beethoven
루트비히 판 베토벤

Biography Comic
who? ㉘ Ludwig van Beethoven

개정판 1쇄 인쇄 2014년 3월　5일
개정판 1쇄 발행 2014년 3월 10일

글 박연아
그림 크레파스
번역 자넷 재완 신
감수 김수희
펴낸이 김선식

책임편집 이유미　**디자인** 박효영
콘텐츠개발팀장 김선영　**콘텐츠개발팀** 박효영, 이유미, 김선민, 조서인
마케팅본부 이상혁

펴낸곳 스튜디오 다산　**출판등록** 2013년 11월 1일 제414-81-37694
주소 경기도 파주시 회동길 37-14 3층
전화 02-702-1724(기획편집) 02-703-1725(마케팅) 02-704-1724(경영관리)
팩스 02-703-2219　**who클럽** cafe.naver.com/dasankids
종이 월드페이퍼(주)　|　**인쇄** (주)현문　|　**제본** 광성문화사

ISBN 979-11-5639-020-6 (14740)

글 **박연아** | 그림 **크레파스** | 번역 **자넷 재완 신** | 감수 **김수희**

Dasan Kid

Ludwig van Beethoven

German musician, December 17, 1770 ~ March 26, 1827

Ludwig van Beethoven is a musician who fought against his own destiny to make great music. When Ludwig was young, his freedom was restricted by his father's strict teaching. Because of his father's selfish motives to raise him to be a prodigy like Mozart and become famous, he spent most of his childhood practicing for recitals.

He eventually even had to quit school. Ludwig learned from a number of teachers, soon demonstrated his musical ability, and started on the path to becoming a musician. Beethoven went to Vienna, the city of music in those days, and met many teachers such as Wolfgang Mozart and Joseph Hayden. There he learned a range of musical genres and refined his skills.

One day as he was slowly becoming known as a performer and writing music on his own, something happened to Beethoven's ears. He tried to hide the fact that he had developed a serious infection in his ears, which would threaten his life as a musician.

But as time passed, his ears grew worse and he eventually lost his hearing completely. Beethoven, however, did not despair at the misfortune of becoming a musician who could not hear, but continued pursuing his music.

During Beethoven's lifespan, he wrote thirty-two piano sonatas and composed many symphonies. Many of his works, such as the Eroica Symphony completed in 1804, the Fate Symphony completed in 1808, and the Choral Symphony composed in 1824, are much admired and considered classics.

Beethoven's music tells us what a true hero is. Just as the hero who overcomes a greater trial shines all the more brighter, Beethoven's music transcends space and time and continues to move people's hearts today.

루트비히 판 베토벤

독일의 음악가, 1770년 12월 17일 ~ 1827년 3월 26일

베토벤은 자신의 운명과 싸워 위대한 음악을 만든 음악가입니다. 베토벤의 어린 시절은 아버지의 엄격한 교육 속에 자유롭지 못했습니다. 모차르트 같은 천재로 키워서 이름을 알리려는 아버지의 그릇된 바람 때문에 베토벤은 어린 시절 대부분의 시간을 연주 연습하는 데 보내야 했습니다.

그리고 결국 학교도 그만두게 되었습니다. 베토벤은 여러 스승의 가르침을 받으며 곧 재능을 발휘하게 되었고 스스로 음악가로서의 길을 가게 되었습니다. 베토벤은 당시 음악의 도시였던 빈에서 모차르트와 하이든을 비롯해 많은 음악의 스승을 만나 다양한 음악의 장르를 배우고 재능을 갈고 닦게 됩니다.

연주자로 조금씩 이름을 알리고 자유롭게 작곡 활동을 하던 어느 날, 베토벤의 귀에 이상이 생겼습니다. 베토벤은 음악가로서의 삶을 위협하는 치명적인 귓병을 사람들에게 숨기기 위해 노력했습니다.

하지만 시간이 갈수록 귓병은 악화되었고 결국 베토벤은 귀가 전혀 들리지 않게 되었습니다. 귀가 들리지 않는 음악가라는 불행 앞에서 베토벤은 좌절하지 않고 음악을 계속했습니다. 자신의 운명과 싸우고 세상을 구원할 영웅을 생각하며 음악을 만들었습니다.

베토벤은 평생에 걸쳐 피아노 소나타 32곡을 만들었고 수많은 교향곡을 작곡했습니다. 1804년에 완성된 〈영웅교향곡〉, 1808년에 완성된 〈운명교향곡〉, 1824년에 완성된 〈합창교향곡〉 등은 지금까지도 고전으로 사랑받고 있습니다.

베토벤의 음악은 사람들에게 진정한 영웅이 무엇인지 알려줍니다. 시련이 클수록 시련을 이겨낸 영웅이 더욱 빛나듯이 그가 남긴 음악은 시공간을 초월해 사람들에게 감동을 전해 주고 있습니다.

이 책을 만든 사람들

글 · 박연아

만화 스토리 작가로 활발하게 활동하고 있습니다. 순정 만화로 시작하여 학습 만화, 창작 만화, 동화까지 작업 범위를 넓혀 왔습니다. 현재는 인물의 어린 시절부터 성공에 이르는 과정을 통해 재미와 감동을 주는 인물 학습 만화 작업에 매진하고 있습니다. 작품으로는 학습 만화『태극 천자문』(1권), 『제중원』, 『화랑세기와 미실』 등이 있습니다. (nicenoel@paran.com)

그림 · 크레파스

어린이들을 위해 새롭고, 재미있고, 즐거운 이야깃거리를 만드는 만화 창작 집단입니다. 세상을 바꾼 인물들의 삶을 통해 어린이들이 희망찬 미래를 만들어가길 바랍니다. 작품으로 『지식 똑똑 경제 리더십 탐구-긍정의 힘』, 『why? 서양 근대 사회의 시작』, 『why? 세계대전과 전후의 세계』 등이 있습니다.

번역 · 자넷 재완 신(Janet Jaywan Shin)

미국 메릴랜드 주에서 태어나고 자랐습니다. 메릴랜드 대학교에서 언어학을 전공하고 UCLA에서 응용언어학 석사 학위를 취득했습니다. 서울대학교 언어교육원에서 전임 강사, 서울대학교 사범대학교 영어교육과에서 초빙교수로 일했습니다. 감수한 책으로『서울대생한테 비밀 영어과외받기』가 있고 고등학교 영어 교과서 교정 작업에 참여했습니다.

감수 · 김수희

연세대학교에서 역사를 전공했습니다. 이후 한국뿐 아니라 일본, 미국에서 한국어, 일본어, 영어를 가르쳐 왔으며 부모를 위한 영어교육용 책을 썼습니다. 영어교육채널 EBSe '엄마표 영어특강'에서 강의를 하며 홈스쿨, 알파벳과 파닉스, 다차원 테마 영어 수업 기법을 알리고 있습니다. 전국 각지에서 어린이 영어 교육에 대한 강연을 하며 창의적이고 열정적인 교수법으로 영어를 배우고자 하는 어린이와 부모들에게 많은 도움을 주고 있습니다.

Ludwig van Beethoven

Ludwig van Beethoven composed only one opera during his time. What is its name?

a. *Fidelio*
b. *Carmen*
c. *Magic Pipe*

Answer: a

Contents

01 Hopes for a Child Prodigy

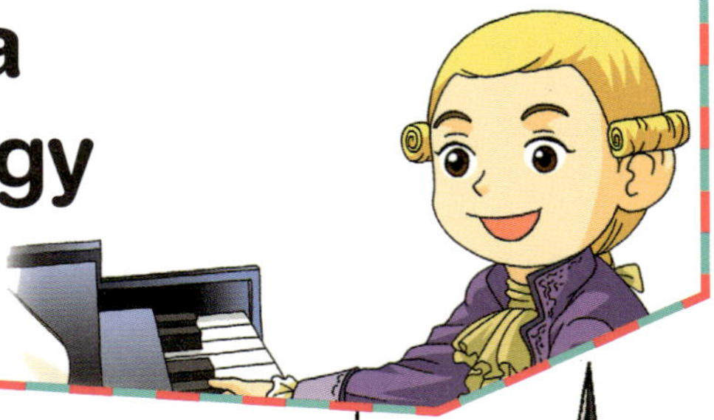

Ludwig van Beethoven was born on December 16, 1770 in Bonn, Germany.

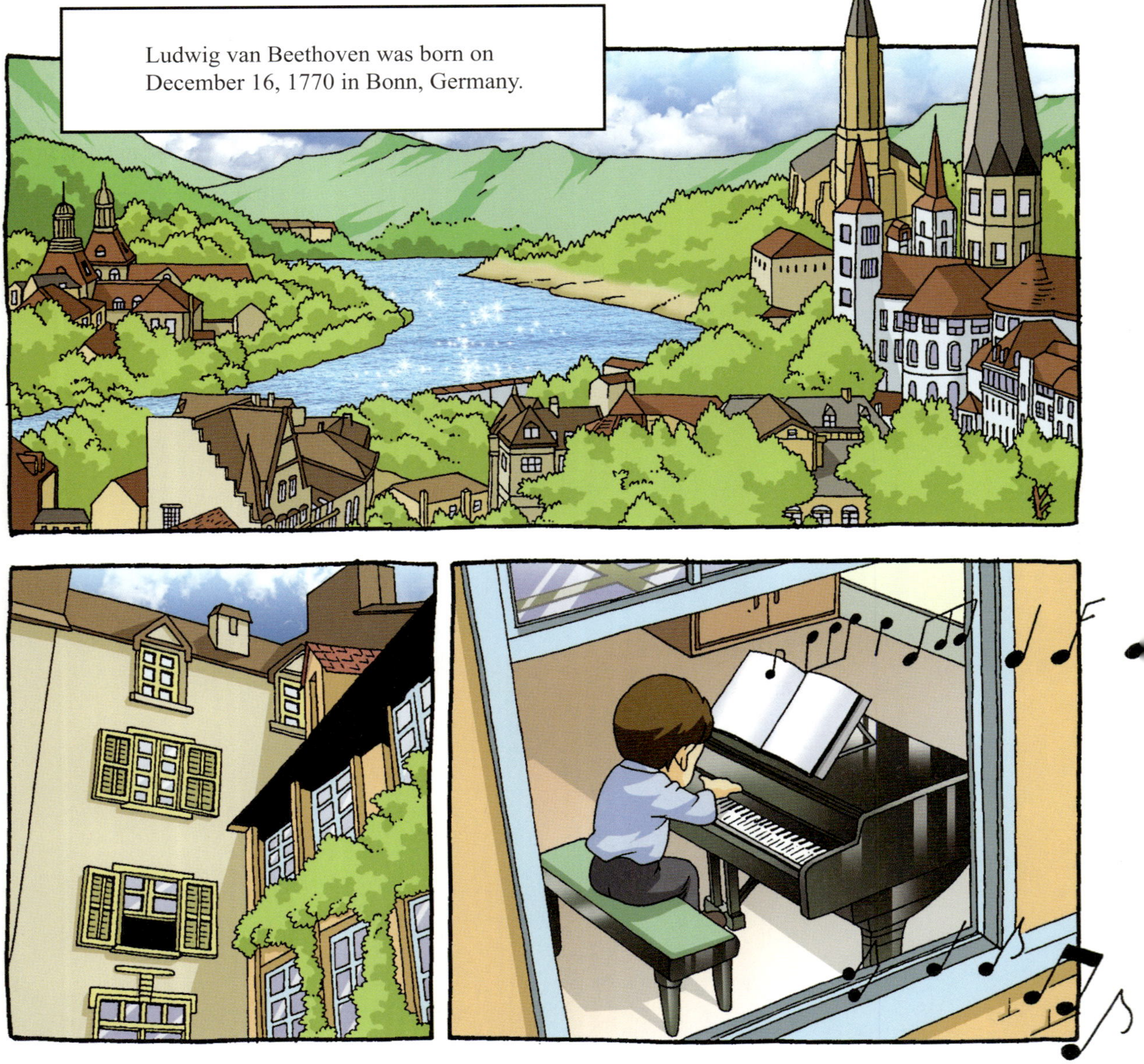

Ludwig's father had followed in his own father's footsteps in becoming a musician of the court as well as being a music teacher. In turn, he also demanded the same of his son, Ludwig.

Stop! Stop!

You still haven't memorized the song? There's a crescendo here! Gradually louder!

And here, each note needs to be distinct!

When Ludwig turned four years old, his father started giving him music lessons and was very strict with him.

What's the use of written music if you're going to play any way you want?

Follow the music!

It's past supper time. He must be quite hungry by now...

Yes, Father.

*crescendo: Musical term meaning to grow gradually louder.

Ludwig's mother, Maria, who was often ill, felt sorry for her son having to undergo his father's harsh music lessons. She could not interfere though because Ludwig's entire education was the responsibility of Johann, his father.

A little faster, with expression!
Ewww, stinky!
Ludwig's dirty.
He must not take a bath very often.
Is it because he's so busy playing piano?
During his elementary school years, Ludwig was just an average child who loved music.

Playing any way you want is not music! Look at the music and play it just as it's written.
I want to play it the way I want.
Why doesn't Father let me play the way I want to play? Practicing the piano would be more fun if I could play however I want...
Aren't you going to go home?
A little later.
I don't want to go home.
...
See you tomorrow then.

Under his father's watchful eye, Ludwig did not have a single moment to rest.

Momma.
I'm scared.
Wrong again! Play it right!
In a few days, Ludwig is going to have a recital.
Make sure he's prepared.
Isn't he too young to have a recital?
He's not too young. Mozart was traveling the world giving concerts at his age!
Dear, Ludwig's age is incorrect on the invitation.
He's eight, but it's written here that he's six.
Whether he's six or eight, he's going to have a recital!
Ludwig's father had subtracted two years from Ludwig's real age so that he could make using his son's talent and bringing fame to his own name.
If he does well at this concert, he'll get so many requests for concerts! Then it's only a matter of time
before we will be raking in the money! Hahaha!

Wake up, Ludwig! You need to shorten your sleeping time so you can practice more. Then people will be calling you a prodigy, just like Mozart!
Can't I sleep just a little more?
To the piano! If you don't, you'll be locked up in the attic!
Mozart, Mozart! I am not Mozart!
I want to play freely! If only I could play this way all the time...

Track 05 ►
?
Why are you playing that kind of garbage? How can you play without any music?
I-I'm sorry, Father.
I told you to practice for the recital. Who said you could play this garbage?
Listen up, Ludwig! I cannot allow you to play whatever you want to play.
Practice for tomorrow's concert!
Hurry up and start!
Yes, sir.
Sob sob...

On March 26, 1778, Ludwig finally held his first recital at the age of eight.

What you just heard was a beautiful aria sung by a singer of the court.

Next,
we have young six-year-old Ludwig van Beethoven playing the piano.

A six-year-old playing a concerto? That's pretty amazing.
He could be a child prodigy like Mozart!

Now, you have nothing to be nervous about. Just play it just like you practiced it.
Yes, sir.
Okay, I'm going to do what Father told me to do. I'll play the music exactly as it's written.

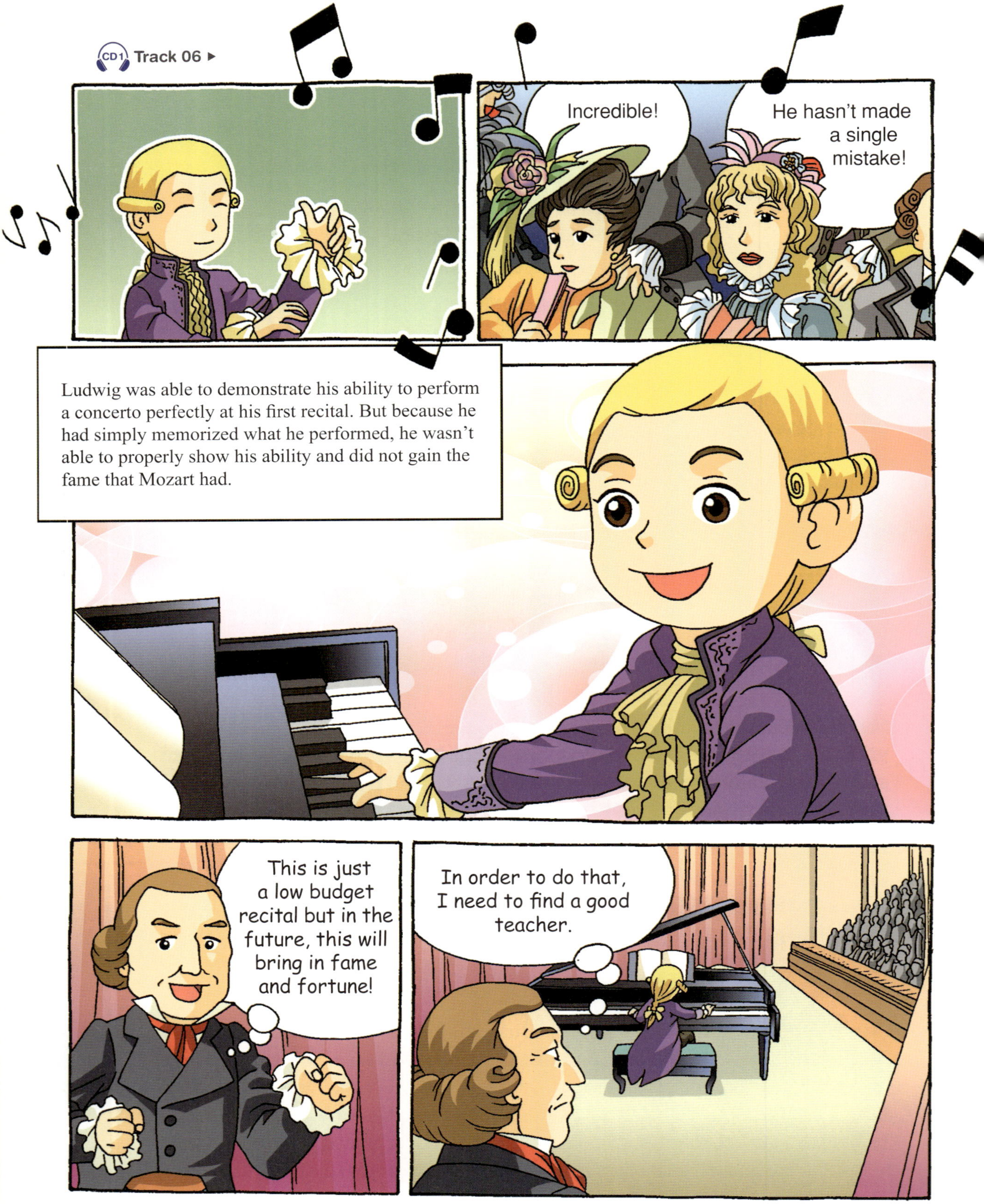

Ludwig was able to demonstrate his ability to perform a concerto perfectly at his first recital. But because he had simply memorized what he performed, he wasn't able to properly show his ability and did not gain the fame that Mozart had.

Say hello to Mr. Eeden. He will be giving you music lessons from now on.
Ludwig's first teacher was Gilles van den Eeden, a court organist.
So you're Ludwig, the one named after your grandfather.
Do you know my grandfather?
Of course, we were friends.
He used to be the Kapellmeister of the court.
When I grow up, I want to be the Kapellmeister of the court, just like my grandfather.
Hahaha. Good.
He had an amiable personality so everyone liked him.
I want to be like that, too.

And your grandfather loved you very much.
That's why he gave me his name.

Ludwig respected his grandfather so much that he kept a portrait of him with him his whole life.

Shall we talk about music now?
Yes!

Your father tells me you're a more of a prodigy than Mozart.
That's his desire.

I'm going to teach you how to play the organ and about the study of harmony.
What's harmony?

The study of harmony is the study of how sounds fit together.

Music is made up of three elements: rhythm, melody, and harmony.

When two or more notes are played at the same time, it's called a chord. Harmony is what happens when the notes of the chord are played together.

If you want to learn how to compose music, this is something you need to learn.

Yes, sir!

Later, whenever the church needed an organist, Eeden would send Ludwig to play. Whenever he got the opportunity, Ludwig would create songs impromptu as he was playing, which his father had always prohibited. During this period, he was able to develop himself musically.

Play whatever you feel like playing as much as you want.

Track 08
His lessons are paying off. If he has several teachers, he'll probably improve his skills even more.
Besides Eeden, Ludwig's father brought home his musician friends to give him more music lessons.
So you're Johann's son, Ludwig. Nice to meet you. Burp!
He will be your music teacher from now on.
Yuck, alcohol smell!
Wake up, Ludwig! Wake up!
Father, can I sleep a little more?
You don't have time to sleep more. Go sit at the piano!
After a late night of drinking, Ludwig's father would often come home and wake him up. Then he would have to practice until morning under the watch of his teacher.
Yes, sir...
Don't fall asleep! Concentrate!

Dear, he hasn't even slept that much...
Do you think just anyone can become a musician of the court?
Don't concern yourself. Just go in and try to sleep.
The teacher has fallen asleep, so go ahead and go to bed.
Yes, Mother.
Ludwig's mother was physically weak and going through many hardships, so she couldn't take care of Ludwig and his siblings very well.
Father won't yell at me?
Your father is sleeping too, so it'll be alright.
Sleep well, Ludwig.
Yes, Mother.
Let me sleep for a while until Father wakes up.

Ludwig, who always appeared disheveled and daydreaming, hardly had any friends. He didn't do well in school either, but he enjoyed going.

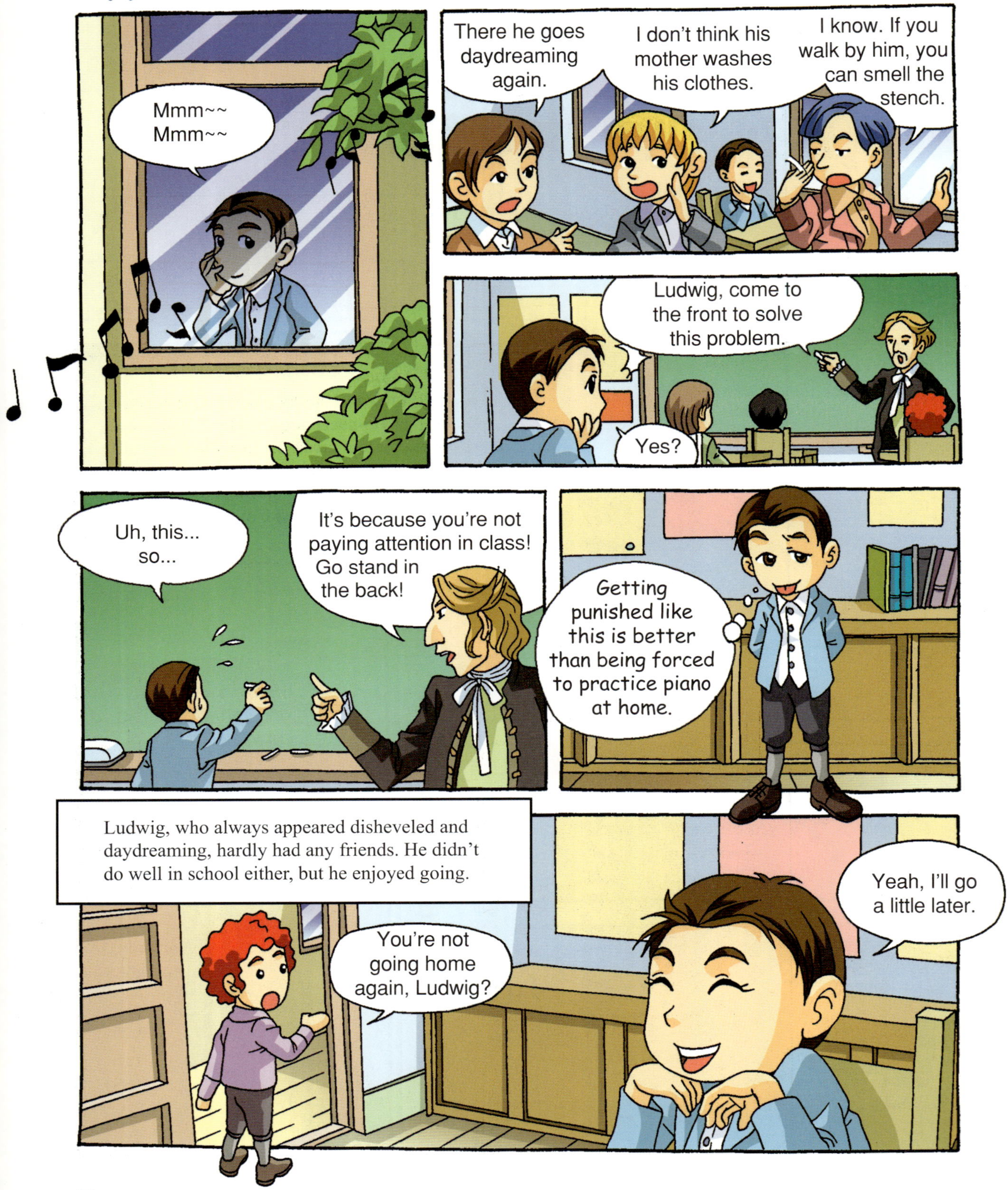

I'm home.
What kept you at school so late?
Uh, well...

Hmph! It's obvious you were just daydreaming at school again.
...
Starting tomorrow, you won't need to go to school anymore.
Excuse me? Why?
Dear!

Ludwig hasn't properly learned how to write yet. He can't stop going to school.
I want to go to school.
If I say stop, you stop!

You're going to be a musician, so you don't need to learn school subjects.
But dear!
I'll go and tell the school myself.
...

Your school grades aren't even very good. It'll be better for you to concentrate on studying music than wasting time in school!
Yes, Father...

Go wash up and sit at the piano!
I can't go to school anymore...

Father is too harsh! I just want to be able to play piano freely... Sob sob.

Ludwig stopped going to school at age 11. For the rest of his life, he had problems with spelling as well as arithmetic.

02 Learning Music Composition

 Track 11 ▶

Yes, Father!
What have you been doing?

Uh...
You were off daydreaming again, weren't you?

Even if you sleep less at night and work harder, I don't think you'll be able to become a court musician!

Do you think I pulled you out of school so that you can daydream?
...

Follow me.
Where are you going?
I'll tell you after I come back.
Sigh.

Hurry up!
...

This day, Ludwig met Christian Gottlob Neefe, the teacher who would have a great influence on his life.
Beautiful!
This man is going to teach you music from now on.
Alright.
This is my son.
Welcome.
Uh..
Nice to meet you, Ludwig.
What are you doing just standing there?
H-hello, Mr. Neefe.

*The Well-Tempered Clavier: A piano instruction book written by Bach for his son and his students.
*clavier: A term referring to keyboard instruments in general, which include the harpsichord, clavichord, and piano.

Ludwig, do you know anything about Bach?
Not really.

Bach is the musician whom I respect the most. You cannot become a true musician without learning about Bach.
Yes, sir!

He is known as the master of harmony. He didn't create a new technique or a new genre, but he would take a piece of music and make it his own. That's why he's called the father of music.

He's well-known for his church music such as the Saint John Passion and the Saint Matthew Passion.
Now, let's see what you can do on the piano.
Can I really play?

Of course! Play to your heart's content.
I'm going to play freely, to my heart's content.

Oh!

When Neefe saw that Ludwig was a prodigy, he decided to help him develop his gift.

Ludwig learned how to compose using works of Bach, who was the master of counterpoint. And this was when Ludwig began to write music on his own.

*counterpoint: A musical technique for composing a piece in which more than two independent melodies are played simultaneously.

This is the first time I've had a student who has made teaching this enjoyable.
I am really lucky to have met Mr. Neefe.
Ludwig, you should be my assistant as the organist of the court.
Excuse me?
If you want to be the organist, you need to work harder than ever.
Yes, sir.
That's right. I'm going to work hard.
It's amazing to see performance with such technique and strength!
Furthermore, he has no problem sight reading a piece he's never seen before.
This child is going to become the next Mozart!

In 1782, at the age of 12, Ludwig became court organist Neefe's assistant. In 1783, he played the cembalo* for the orchestra. This was a big responsibility as it involved playing the keyboard instrument as well as conducting the orchestra.

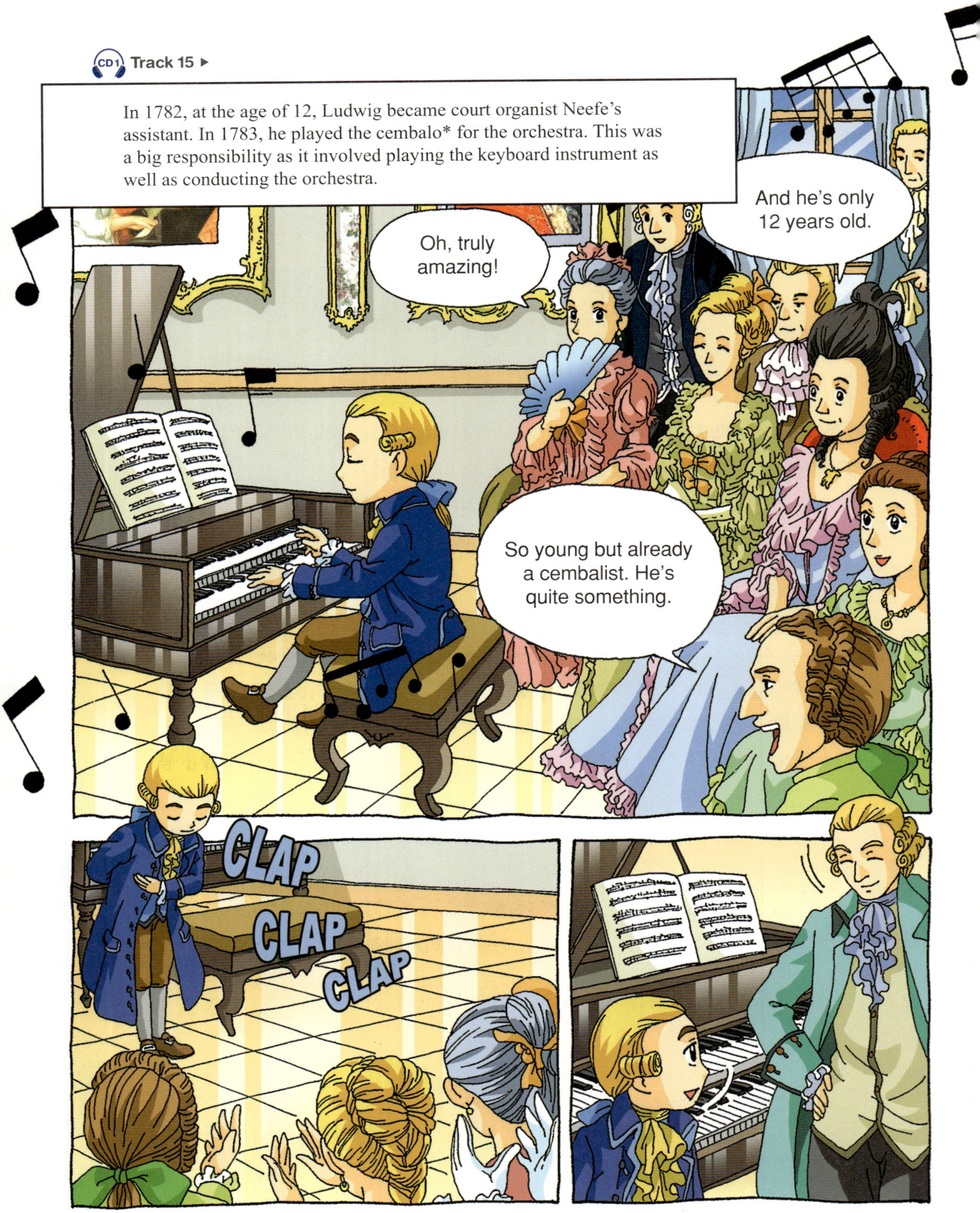

*cembalo: A keyboard instrument which produces vibrant tones using picks to pluck strings, instead of hammers to hit strings like in a piano. It was used primarily during the sixteenth through eighteenth century.

Ludwig's father would sometimes hold recitals in his home for a fee. Many people from noblemen to university people to government officials would attend and Ludwig became even more famous.

I will let you know when there will be another recital.
Hey! What brings you here so late at night?
Listen, Johann!
Do you think I can sleep with all this noise? How can you invite strangers into the house almost every night and hold recitals without my permission as your landlord?
Come now, let it go. What are friends for, right? Whenever you want to hear my son play, just let me know anytime.
Can you hold the recitals less frequently? There are too many.
Between friends, can't you be more understanding?
What's going on? Cough cough.
SLAM
All he thinks about is money!
It's nothing. Don't worry about it. Go in and get some rest.

Ludwig! Ludwig!
He's probably tired. Just let him rest.
Do not meddle.
Did you call me, Father?
You know that your mother is very ill, don't you? Her medicine costs quite a bit. Just to let you know, we're going to hold more recitals from now on.
Yes, sir.
Are you going out?
Don't worry about where I'm going!
If only your father didn't drink, our budget wouldn't be so tight... His salary goes straight to his alcohol. It's going to be hard on you.
COUGH
COUGH
It's alright. Your health improving is what's important.
Don't worry about money. I will take care of everything.
I'm sorry, son.
But you need to hurry and get better.

Track 17

Ludwig's father's wages from the court, combined with the money Ludwig earned from his recitals, was enough to support the family. But after the earl who was Johann van Beethoven's benefactor died, Johann's alcoholism grew worse day by day. As a result, Ludwig's mother needed to start working and earn money.

You're going to work today, too?

Thanks to you, I've gotten a lot better. Cough, cough.

The death of the earl, Father's benefactor, was a major shock for Father.

I don't know how we are going to get by with him getting drunk every night and not taking care of the family.

Alright, I'll be back later.

All of our money has been spent and Mother cannot earn enough by herself. We're going to end up starving at this rate. I'm going to write to the Elector!

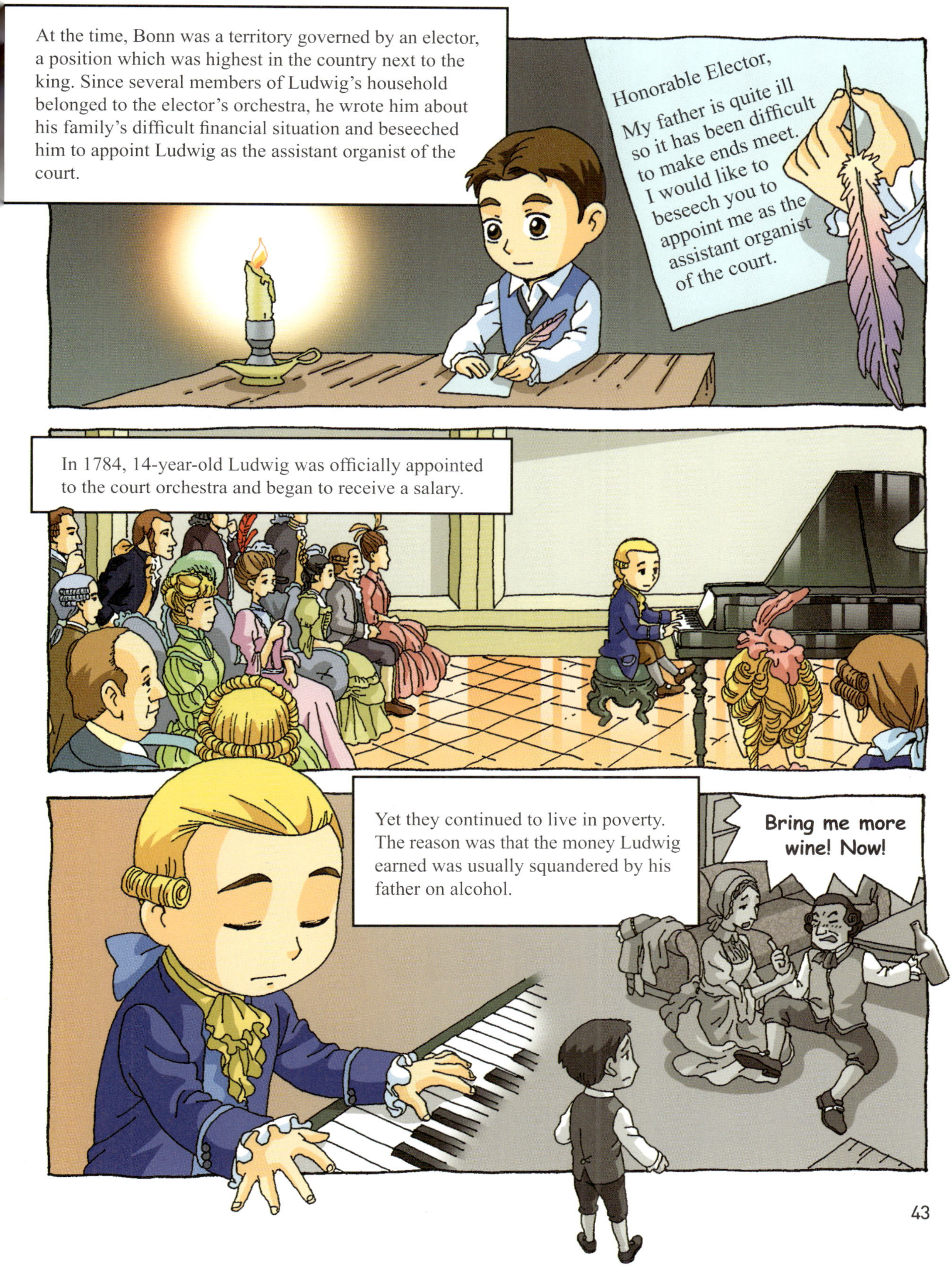

At the time, Bonn was a territory governed by an elector, a position which was highest in the country next to the king. Since several members of Ludwig's household belonged to the elector's orchestra, he wrote him about his family's difficult financial situation and beseeched him to appoint Ludwig as the assistant organist of the court.

In 1784, 14-year-old Ludwig was officially appointed to the court orchestra and began to receive a salary.

Yet they continued to live in poverty. The reason was that the money Ludwig earned was usually squandered by his father on alcohol.

43

Neefe helped Ludwig to develop depth in his musical talent. His efforts allowed Ludwig to be greatly influenced by Mozart's music which was expressive and full of life.

Ah, the melody is so clear and vivid. I can feel Mozart's free spirit. Anyone can recognize that this is the music of Wolfgang Mozart!

I can understand the reason why Mozart's music is praised.

His music is special!

I want to be recognized for my music, too.

Ludwig was greatly influenced by Bach and Mozart. His own composing skills were not fully developed yet, but he did start publishing songs.

He's playing Mozart's piece.
My word, this child has already surpassed me. I don't think I have anything more to teach him.
Besides Wolfgang Mozart, there is no one who is able to teach him.

Beethoven! Beethoven!
Franz! What are you doing here?
Well...
What's going on?
Your mother...
What?
...was having severe coughing fits when she suddenly collapsed.
Ludwig's mother, who was his sole source of comfort, was gradually getting worse in terms of her health.
Ludwig, I'm sorry that I couldn't take better care of you.
Mother, you can't go yet!

Studying Humanities

Is she alright?
Yeah, she's much better.
Franz Wegeler was a medical student but he and Ludwig shared a deep friendship and were close their whole life.
That's good.
I'm writing music to make into a book, but it's not enough.
I have to find more work.
The von Breuning family is looking for a piano teacher. Are you interested?
Do you think I can?
I've never taught anyone before...
Let's go there right now.
The mistress of the house will see you shortly.
Thank you.
Don't you think I'm too young to be a teacher? I don't think I'll get the job.
At least give it a try.

Is the new piano teacher coming, Mother?
That's what I'm told.

Good afternoon, ma'am.
Welcome.
Good afternoon. My name is Ludwig van Beethoven.

You look like you're the same age as me.
You look too young to be a teacher.
Hmm~

Nice to meet you, Mr. Beethoven.
Uh, yes...

We look forward to your lessons.
Welcome, sir.

Uh, yes...
Good luck.

Wegeler introduced his good friend, Ludwig, as a piano teacher to the von Breunings, an aristocratic family he was acquainted with. While Ludwig taught the von Breuning children piano, he was able to learn literature and etiquette from them.

May I ask what you are doing?
There are so many books here. I was just looking at the titles.

There are two things that people in our family like. One is music and the other is books.

What are you two doing? Heh heh.
Let's start our lesson!

What song are we learning today?

What? Where is all of our money?
What money are you talking about?
You don't think I know that Ludwig is making a hefty salary?
All of it is being spent on your drinking, so there's none in our savings!
Hmph! I'm supposed to believe that?
See? Here it is. You're still going to say we don't have any money? Hahaha!
Ludwig!
What's going on?

Ludwig's father's alcoholism grew worse as time passed. Eventually, because of his addiction, he could no longer work for the court, and Ludwig had to take on the responsibility of providing for the family.

Ludwig had published about ten pieces of music already, but after he took on the full responsibility of providing for his family, he hardly had time to compose for four years, starting from 1785.
I now no longer have anything more to teach you.
Sir...
So I invited Mr. Mozart. The only one who can teach you is Mozart.
Mr. Mozart!
In 1786, Neefe gave Ludwig the opportunity to go to Vienna, a bigger place where he could expand his musical skills.
Vienna?
Ludwig, I want you to see more of the world out there.
How would you like to go to Vienna?

I've put in my recommendation for you already. The Elector will cover the expenses.
Go and meet Mr. Mozart.
It feels like a dream to be able to go to Vienna, where the artistic world lives and breathes.
Live out your dream to the fullest in Vienna.
Vienna, the city of music. A place all musicians must visit at least once in their lifetime!
I can't believe I'm going to Vienna!
I can probably meet great musicians like Mozart and Hayden there.
In 1787, Ludwig left Bonn, Germany, and headed for Vienna, a place where operas and concerts abound, the city of music and culture and the center of the classical music world.

Finally, the day I get to meet Wolfgang Mozart!
I'm so nervous at the thought of actually meeting him in person!

What will he think of my playing?

My name is Ludwig van Beethoven from Bonn. I've come to see Mr. Mozart.

Sir, you have a visitor from Bonn.

From Bonn?
Oh, yes. So you're Ludwig.
It is an honor to meet you.
Your reputation in Bonn is quite well-known. Would you like to play a piece?
Yes, sir.
Ludwig van Beethoven and Wolfgang Mozart met for the first time that day. 17-year-old Ludwig did his best to demonstrate his skills to the greatest musician of that time period.
Who is that?
I heard he's a musician from Bonn.
There is something different about this young man!
Wow, his skills are quite something.
Hmm, you have great skills.
Thank you, sir.
But anyone who practices enough can reach this level of playing.

Do you know how many aspiring musicians come here every day?
Please give me another chance.
If you choose a song for me, I will sight read it.
This is part of a piece I'm working on right now, called Don Giovanni.

He's playing a piece that he's never seen before so effortlessly!
This young man is a natural-born musician!
Attention, everyone!
Remember the name Ludwig van Beethoven. This young man is going to amaze the world some day!
Thank you, sir.

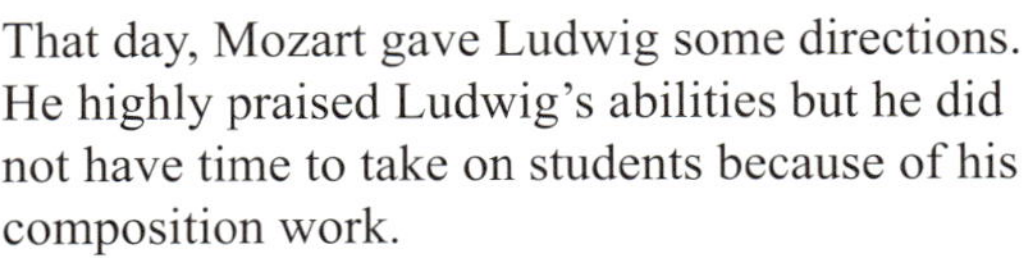

That day, Mozart gave Ludwig some directions. He highly praised Ludwig's abilities but he did not have time to take on students because of his composition work.

After only two weeks in Vienna, Ludwig received word that his mother was in critical condition and returned to Bonn.

Mother, please wait just a little longer!

Mother!

I'm here now. Please get better.

You worked so hard to be able to study overseas. I'm sorry I can't help you. Cough cough.

Ludwig, I don't think I have much longer to live. I'm afraid that I have to ask you to take care of your younger brothers.

Stay strong. You are going to get better soon, Mother.

Not long after Ludwig returned from Vienna, his mother who was suffering from tuberculosis breathed her last breath. He fell into deep despair when his mother, who had always been his supporter, passed away.

Mother, you were my dearest friend. I will no longer have anyone to call 'Mother.'

Overwhelmed by the sadness of losing his mother, the responsibility of providing for his family, and harassment from his alcoholic father, Ludwig fell into depression and wrote only one piece in four years.

In 1788, 18-year-old Ludwig was introduced to Count Ferdinand von Waldstein by the von Breuning family. Waldstein was only about nine years older than Beethoven, but from that day on, they became close friends and he became one of Beethoven's financial supporters.

This young man is Ludwig van Beethoven. He's a court musician.
Nice to meet you. I'm Ferdinand Waldstein.
Nice to meet you, Count Waldstein.
The Count has an extensive knowledge about music.
You flatter me, Mrs. von Breuning.
Would you like to hear Ludwig play, Count?
It would be an honor for me.
If someone like him could appreciate my music, that would be great.
Mr. Beethoven's performances are always so powerful!
Shhh!

Count Waldstein fell in love with Ludwig van Beethoven's music after hearing him perform that day. From this point on, he became Beethoven's supporter and gave much help to him both mentally and financially.

In July, 1789, a huge wave swept over all of Europe called the French Revolution. Through the acquaintance of Count Waldstein, Ludwig became interested in politics, not to mention science and philosophy. He was able to attend philosophy classes at the University of Bonn and increase his knowledge of the humanities. Beethoven who became exposed to the study of humanities developed depth in his world of music.

Today's lecture on the revolution was perfectly fitting for Professor Schneider, who is a revolutionary.
A revolution for freedom and equality! There's a beauty in the revolution.
Hahaha! We have ourselves a revolutionary right here.
Ludwig did not like the class-based society in which aristocrats ruled and the king was the central power. As he listened to his friend Eulogius Schneider's lecture, he became filled with passion for the revolution.
Everyone is equal. The monarchy needs to be done away with!
The power to change the world! That's why a revolution is so great!
During this period, Ludwig also read the works of German philosopher Johann Wolfgang von Goethe and playwright and poet Friedrich Schiller, all of which greatly influenced his later composition works.
I want to make revolutionary music!

Vienna, City of Music

CD1 **Track 30** ▶

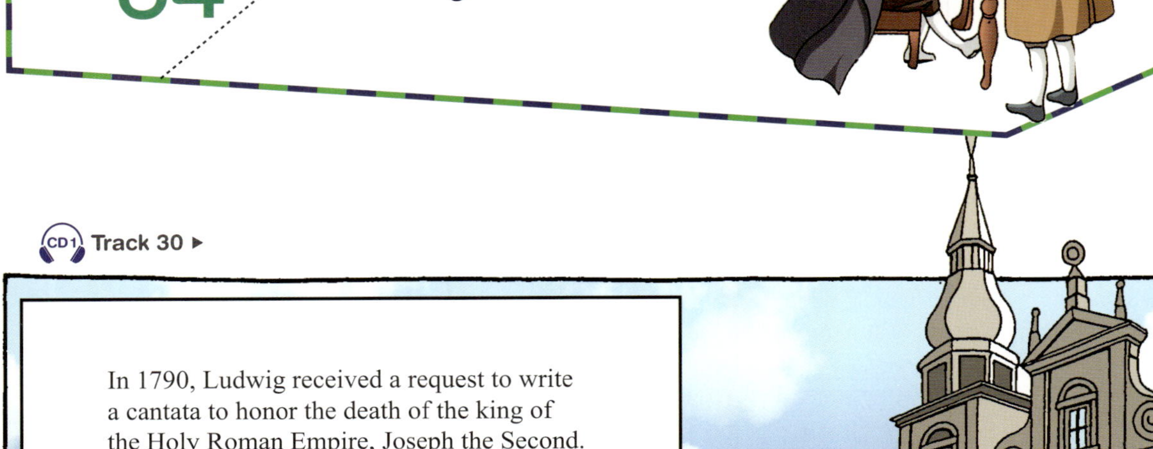

Through his friendship with Schneider, Ludwig was asked to write a cantata for the king. He put all of his heart into it as he mourned the death of his personal hero and completed the piece. However, the piece was so difficult to play that it was not performed in his lifetime.

CD1 Track 31 ▶
In 1792, Joseph Hayden attended a concert performed on his behalf by the Bonn court orchestra. It was here that Ludwig's destiny crossed paths with Hayden.
It is an honor to meet you, Mr. Hayden.
Welcome.
It is such a shame that Mozart has died at the age of 35.
Vienna is in a state of shock. They are eagerly waiting for another musician to take his place.
Ludwig!
Yes, sir.
This young man is my student, Ludwig van Beethoven.
This is the young man whose piano skills are so outstanding.
I have wanted to meet you, too.
It is an honor, Mr. Hayden.

These are pieces that I composed.
Ah, this is a cantata to commemorate King Joseph's death.

He demonstrates a strong distinct style of his own!
It's not perfect, but this is something else!

Would you be interested in studying under me? Come with me to Vienna.
Excuse me?
Another chance has come for me to fulfill my dreams in Vienna!
Mother, I'm going to Vienna to become a great musician.

Congratulations, Ludwig!
This is a good opportunity.
But...
Ludwig, what are you hesitating for?
This is what you've always wanted, isn't it?
Yes, this is what I've always wished for. Now the time has come.
Don't worry about your younger brothers. I will help them.
The Elector is going to financially support you. Go back to Vienna and show the world your talent!
Yes, I'll go to Vienna.

Take care, Johann, Carl. Count Waldstein and Mr. Neefe are going to take good care of you.

Once I get settled in Vienna, you have to come visit.

I'm worried because I think Father is quite ill.

Father...

I'm sorry. I can't give up my dream this time. Please take care of Father for me.

Ludwig finally left Bonn and headed for Vienna in high spirits.

I'm going to become the Vienna court concert master before I return!

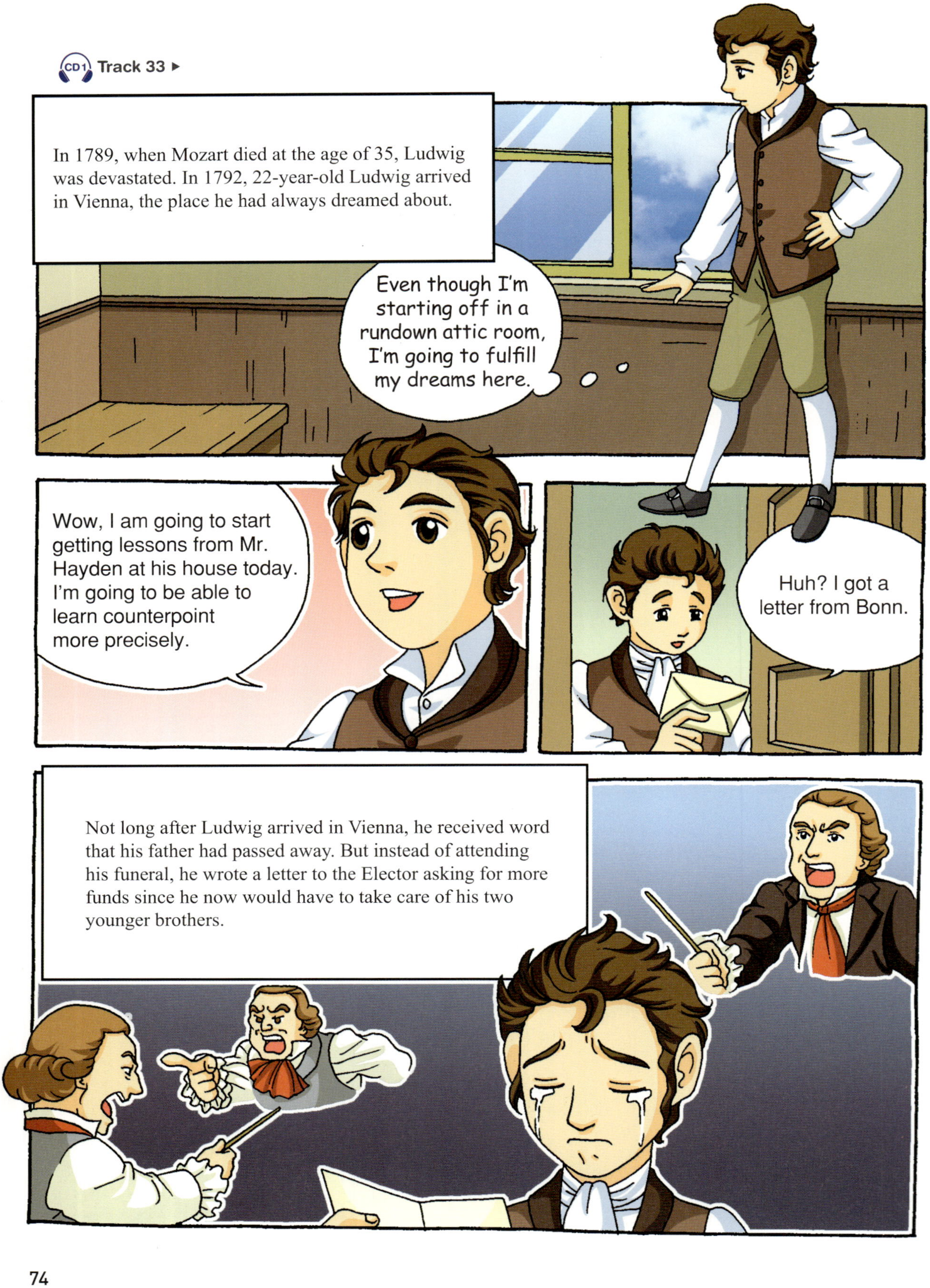

In 1789, when Mozart died at the age of 35, Ludwig was devastated. In 1792, 22-year-old Ludwig arrived in Vienna, the place he had always dreamed about.

Not long after Ludwig arrived in Vienna, he received word that his father had passed away. But instead of attending his funeral, he wrote a letter to the Elector asking for more funds since he now would have to take care of his two younger brothers.

Ludwig looked forward to learning more about counterpoint, a composition technique, from Joseph Hayden. However Hayden did not have any time to teach Ludwig because of the many social gatherings and concerts he had to attend.
Let's end the lesson here for today.
Is there anything I should work on?
Well, it sounded fine to me.
I completed the assignment you gave me. Could you take a look?
He didn't cover anything today either. How am I going to learn anything this way?
I'm very busy today, so I'll look at it at your next lesson.
Yes, sir.
Mr. Hayden has absolutely no time to help me with my music studies because of his busy schedule.
At this rate, I'm just going to waste my time here in Vienna and not learn anything.

Ludwig already had a reputation from his days in Bonn as an outstanding pianist. Consequently, he would get many invitations to play at the mansion or salon of noblemen. He would also frequently go to social gatherings in order to find more supporters.
I don't think there are any musicians as good as Mozart.
All of the decent pianists have left Vienna altogether.
Woelfel, who was a student of Mozart's father, performs in Warsaw, I heard.
Apparently, there aren't any true musicians left in Vienna.
Well, it appears that all of the people who had some musicianship have left Vienna.
This is Ludwig van Beethoven, from Bonn!
We will begin the performance.

What kind of performance is this? I can't bear to listen to this.
It's rough but I like it.
It's rare to see this kind of intense playing.
Contrary to the popular music style of that time, which was light and delicate, Ludwig's music was intense and intricate. The musicians and young aristocrats who heard his playing that day were deeply moved.
Wow, absolutely captivating.
This is an incredible performance. He's a student of Hayden, isn't he?
Mozart doesn't even compare to him.
I've got to prove my worth here in Vienna through my style of music.
That guy's amazing. Our jobs could be at stake.
But let's compare properly.

I'm Daniel Steibelt. I would like to challenge you to an improvisation contest some time.
I will gladly accept whenever you invite me.

I've got to establish my place in Vienna with a performance that exceeds everyone else's!

Some time later, Ludwig participated in an improvisation contest with Steibelt.
Ah, his performance brings peace to the soul.

There, now it's your turn to perform.
Alright.
Wh-what?

He's playing so fast you can hardly sense his hands moving.
There's no way I can beat that.
How can he play spontaneously like that?

That was a truly remarkable performance. Hayden must be so proud of you.
Well, I don't know.

Mr. Hayden is so busy that he hardly has time to teach me.
There is no use in continuing to meet with him.

How can he not have time to teach a young man with this much talent?
That's too bad.

Why don't you come by my house some time?
Yes, sir.

Track 36

Steibelt felt pity for the fact that Ludwig couldn't get much musical training from Hayden. Consequently, he introduced him to a musician he knew named Schenk to give him guidance.

Oh, unbelievable!

It's been a long time since I've felt this way.

Isn't it a pity to let Beethoven go untrained, not learning anything from Hayden?

Hmm...

I will teach you counterpoint instead of Hayden.

If you are willing to teach me, I will work very hard.

But there is one condition.

I will do that.

You must keep it a secret from Mr. Hayden.

Ludwig learned counterpoint from Schenk which he was not able to learn from Hayden.

Ludwig, you really disappoint me!
The music you gave me weren't pieces you composed here but ones you had already composed back in Bonn! How could you deceive me like that?
Well, uh...
Moreover, you're learning about counterpoint from Schenk? And you kept it a secret from me.
Uh...
The rumors are widespread!
Steibelt must've been telling everyone.
In 1793, Hayden became extremely angry when he found out that the works that Ludwig was showing him as pieces he had just composed were actually pieces he had composed back in Bonn. In addition, he learned that Ludwig was learning counterpoint from Schenk.
Let's reconsider the performance tour to London. You may leave now.
Yes, sir.

*op.: opus. An expression indicating the number of a musical work.

But about the third piece...
Yes, sir. Is there a problem?
The third piece is too difficult to play so I think it would be better not to publish that one.
That's the one I like the most. Don't publish it?
With that one omitted, it's perfect!
I don't understand
That one got the best response by far. Why exclude it? I'm sure that Mr. Hayden is saying that because he is jealous!
Later in the future, Hayden explains that he didn't know that the trio he criticized would be so quickly accepted by the general public. But Ludwig could not forgive Hayden that easily.
Mr. Hayden thought that my creative ability was limited.
He basically looked down on me as a musician.
Even though he's my teacher, I cannot forgive him!

Oh, there you are, Mr. Beethoven. That was a fabulous performance.
Every time I hear you perform, it moves me.
I'm grateful that you enjoy my performance, Prince and Princess Lichnowsky.

A person who creates music must travel often in order to be inspired to write new songs. Let's go travel somewhere
together when we have the chance.
Oh, that is a splendid idea. Hoho.
I am going to keep composing for people who appreciate my music.

Lichnowsky held a recital every Friday. The Prince who highly valued Ludwig's musical talent introduced him to many noblemen and encouraged them to support him.

Prince and Princess Lichnowsky certainly do love Ludwig van Beethoven.
The Prince used to be a student of Mozart. What a discerning ear he must have for music.
It must be great to be under the same roof as such a great musician.

During this period, Ludwig began to become known not only as a pianist but also as a composer. His work published as number one, the *Three Piano Trios (op.1)*, received much praise, with the third piece in C minor receiving a phenomenal response.

As a result of this course of events, Ludwig's relationship with Hayden became more distant, and Hayden ended up going to London alone for the performance tour they had planned on going on together.

Ludwig was able to get regular lessons on counterpoint from Johann Albrechtsberger, a composer and teacher whom Hayden introduced to him.

05 A Heartbreaking Destiny

CD 2 Track 01 ▶

Ludwig was being cared for by the Prince and Princess as he worked on his music. But as their affection became excessive, thoughts of wanting to leave became stronger.

In 1794, France occupied up to the Rhine River in Germany and Ludwig was not able to fulfill his dream to become concert master and return to Bonn. At this time, his brother Carl came to Vienna.

In 1795, Ludwig's youngest brother, Johann, came to Vienna and worked as a pharmacist. Later he opened his own pharmacy and settled down in Vienna.

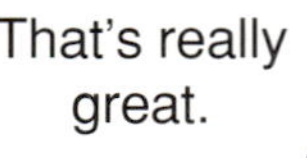

Ludwig's reputation as a composer was not as strong as his reputation as a pianist, but from this point on, his ability to compose began to stand out.
Sir, representatives from publishing companies are here.
I told you not to bother me when I'm working!
You may not enter right now.
Please just give us a few minutes.
Not now, I said!
What is it?
We want to publish the work that you recently composed!
What are you talking about? We were here first!
Mr. Beethoven! Let us publish it!
Get out of here!
When the piece is finished, I will announce it, so get out!
SLAM
Stop cutting in line!
I came here first!
Mr. Beethoven! Please open the door.

It was during this period that Ludwig first presented himself in a concert to the public as both a pianist and composer.
I heard this is the first time he is performing in a concert the work he composed himself.
I heard that he finished writing the piano concerto he's going to perform today just two days ago.
Oh, it's about to begin.
This piece is in C major, but this piano is a half step flat, so...
On this day, the piano used for the concert was a half step flat, so Ludwig changed the piece to C# major and played the C major piece with seven sharps.

The concert in which Ludwig's ability shined ended successfully, and everyone complimented him profusely.

From February to July, 1796, Ludwig went on a performance tour with Prince Lichnowsky and was very popular.

He performed one of the pieces he had composed himself, a cello sonata, before the King of Germany Frederich Wilhelm II and received much praise.

I will never be able to forget my time in Germany for as long as I live. This performance tour was truly incredible!

Judging from your face, you seem to have had a really good time.
It was amazing. I got a warm reception from everyone who was a music lover.

Haha. With your music, they would.
Huh? What did you say?

With your music, everyone would've liked it!
Whoa!

What is this? Something is wrong with my ears.

Ludwig's problems with his hearing began in the prime of his composing days, at the age of 26.
The ringing in my ears has stopped! Was it because I drank too much?

The ringing in his ears continued, so he sought a doctor.
Hmm. As of now, it's hard to know the reason for the ringing.
Is that bad? There's nothing wrong with my ears, is there?
When I'm in a loud environment, I can't hear high pitches.
It could be a temporary problem and improve again.
For the time being, refrain from alcohol and I would also recommend resting at a nearby hot springs.
After some time has passed, I will reexamine your ears.
Alright. Thank you.
There's probably nothing major wrong with my ears. The doctor said it could get better.
Right, it's probably nothing. It'll be fine.

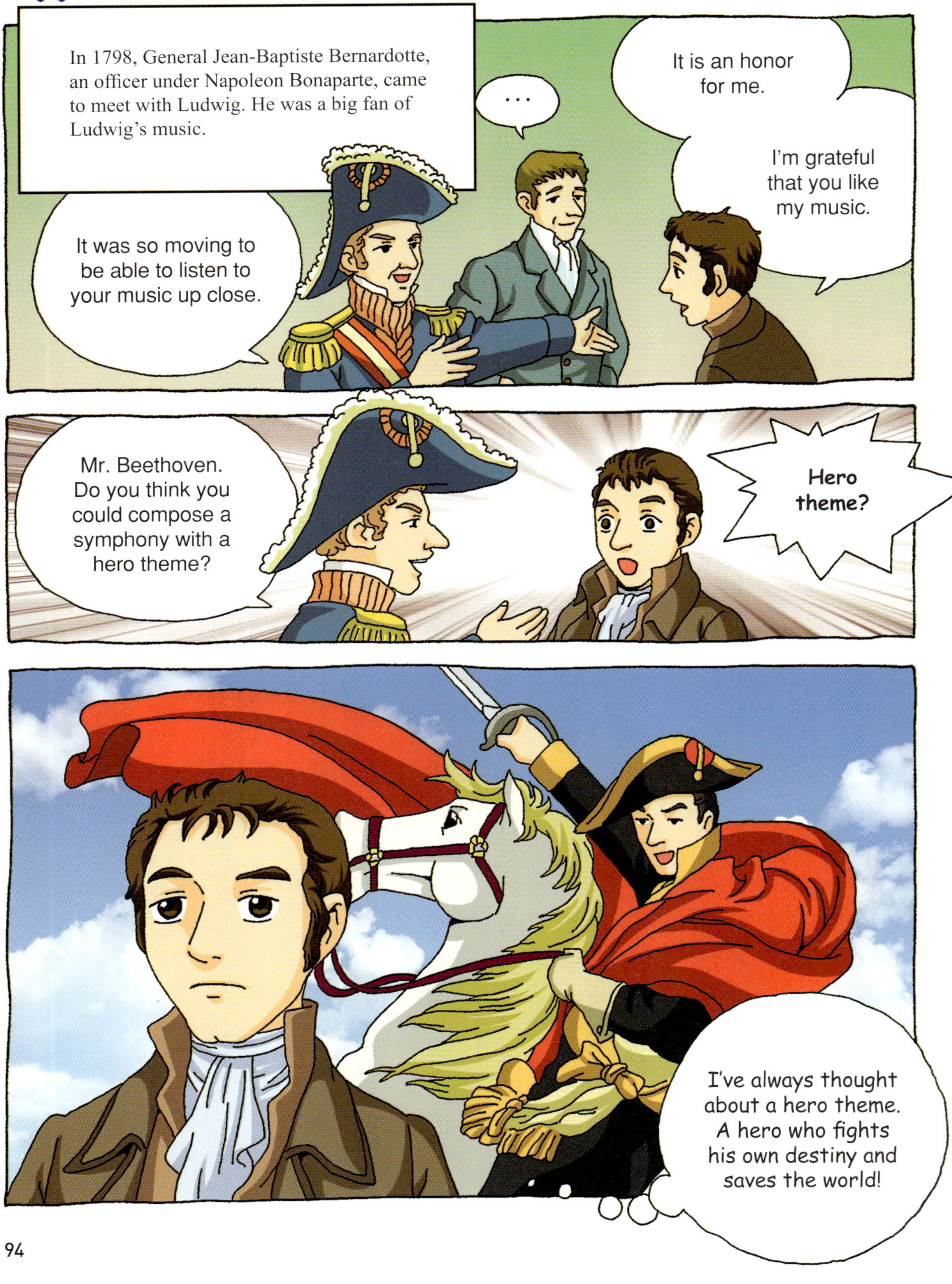

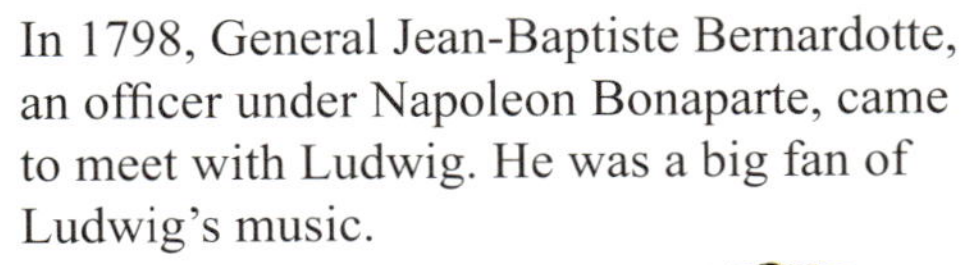

In 1798, General Jean-Baptiste Bernardotte, an officer under Napoleon Bonaparte, came to meet with Ludwig. He was a big fan of Ludwig's music.

Ludwig accepted General Bernardotte's request and worked hard on the piece in the midst of a busy schedule full of concerts.

Have you heard of someone named Woelfel?
Woelfel? People talked about him being a child prodigy who performed at concerts at the age of seven.

That Woelfel has challenged you to an improvisation contest.
Apparently, he wants to compare our abilities.

Sounds amusing.
This is not the time to joke around.
Woelfel has an overwhelming number of people rooting for him.

That doesn't matter. I play for people who understand my music and accept it.
I don't want to force my music on people who can't feel my music with their hearts.
I'm looking forward to the challenge.

CD2 Track 06 ▶

Many people gathered together to watch the improvisation contest between Ludwig and Woelfel.

I'm very excited to see this contest between these two people.

We will know the results very soon.

I can't believe I get to see an improvisation contest between two famous musicians. It's like a dream come true!

Who will win?

Woelfel's performance is always graceful.

It gives one a sense of delicate pleasure.

I like the fact that Woelfel's playing is easy to listen to.

Now it is time to hear Mr. Beethoven's performance.

Why is he so arrogant?
Just like people say, he doesn't have any manners.
He's not known to be bad-tempered for no reason.
Alright everyone, let's stop and listen. Let's see how he performs.

CD 2 Track 07
How does he do it?
It's so rough! How is anyone moved by that kind of music?
But his music is stirring people's emotions.
You can't really listen to Beethoven's music properly without first opening your heart.

My ears!

Oh, for a moment, I couldn't hear a thing.
WOW

Yeah, I must've been mistaken just now.
It just went quiet for a moment, that's all.
I scared myself thinking I lost my hearing! But now I can hear perfectly.

I was overly sensitive yesterday.
But why is it so quiet outside?

Why does everything sound so quiet?

I think my ears have gotten worse starting some time ago. I've got to keep it a secret from people.
If people find out I went to see a doctor because of my hearing, that could be the end of my career as a musician.

These days, I hear the ringing in my ears more frequently.
I don't know if my ears have gotten more sensitive, but I often feel pain, too.
This doesn't mean that I might lose my hearing, does it?
Hmm...

You should get some rest in a quiet place.
Because of this problem with your ears, both your body and your mind are under stress.
In this condition, your ears could get worse.
Really?

If my ears get worse, does that mean I could become deaf?
After I finish this next concert and wrap up some other things, I'll look for a place to go take a rest.

Birth of a Hero

I would like to study under you, Mr. Forster.
Come on in.
From now on, you are going to study the process of composing a quartet with me.
As Ludwig studied under an outstanding composing teacher named Forster, he continued to improve his composing skills through interaction with other musicians such as Johann Albrechsberger and Antonio Salieri.
In addition, he later taught Carl Czerny, who would become widely known for his piano teaching books.

Until then, musicians would sell their songs for the price that publishers set. But in 1801, Ludwig became the first musician to set the price of his own work when *The Creatures of Prometheus* became recognized all over and foreign publishers were fiercely competing for it.

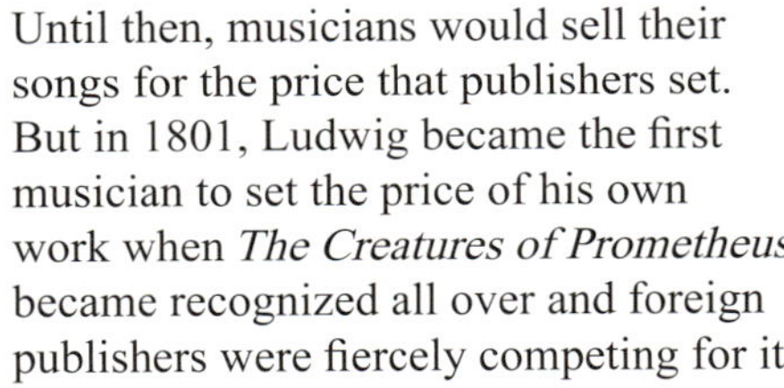

*ducat: An old European unit of currency.

To my friend Franz,

These days everything is going well. But my hearing has been getting worse for the past three years. In addition, I have a constant ringing in my ears day and night, which prevents me from sleeping. I'm living a quite miserable life.

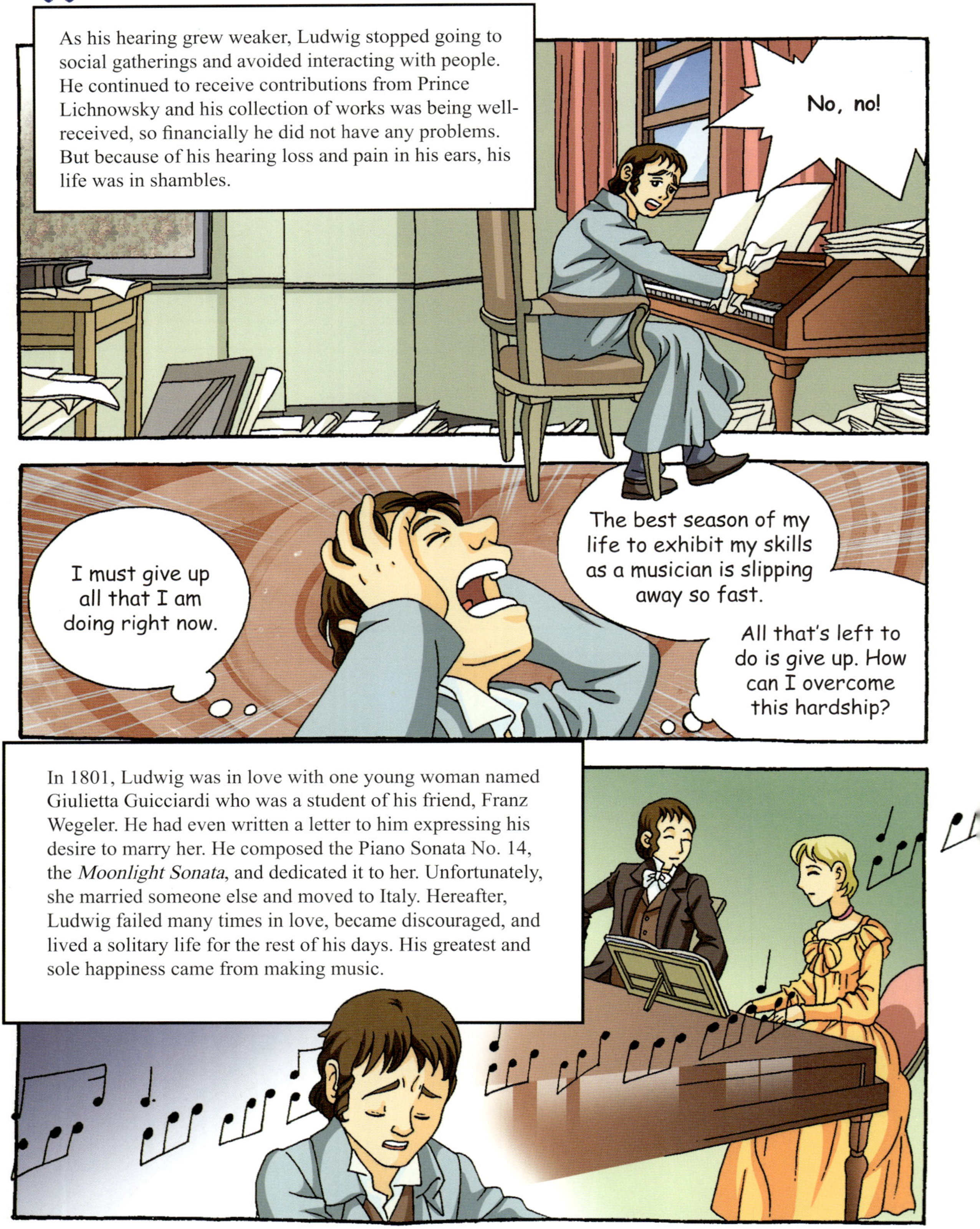

As his hearing grew weaker, Ludwig stopped going to social gatherings and avoided interacting with people. He continued to receive contributions from Prince Lichnowsky and his collection of works was being well-received, so financially he did not have any problems. But because of his hearing loss and pain in his ears, his life was in shambles.

In 1801, Ludwig was in love with one young woman named Giulietta Guicciardi who was a student of his friend, Franz Wegeler. He had even written a letter to him expressing his desire to marry her. He composed the Piano Sonata No. 14, the *Moonlight Sonata*, and dedicated it to her. Unfortunately, she married someone else and moved to Italy. Hereafter, Ludwig failed many times in love, became discouraged, and lived a solitary life for the rest of his days. His greatest and sole happiness came from making music.

As Ludwig's hearing worsened, he actually became even more absorbed in writing new music and living inside his music world. An old musician friend from Bonn, Antoni Reicha, came to Vienna.
Welcome, Anton.
You've gotten thin, my friend.

I'm thinking of leaving the city soon to spend some time in a quieter place.
Good. Getting some rest is not a bad idea.

I wanted to ask you if you wrote this piece. I was wondering because some parts of it were a bit strange.
What?

This is my work but it's been altered. The publishers just edit it any way they want!
Don't be too upset. Actually, publishers edit without the composer's permission all the time.
I cannot accept this! I clearly told them before publishing that they must not change this part in any way without my permission! Those deceitful liars! They will not hear the end of this!

When Ludwig discovered the fact that his work was edited without permission before being published, he became furious. He then published a statement expressing his opinion in a newspaper called the Wiener Zeitung.

Wiener Zeitung
It is my responsibility to disclose the fact that this is not the original work but an imitation created by the publisher. The publisher needs to stop tarnishing the reputation of composers and deceiving the general public. They must clearly state the truth on their book covers. I plan to publish my future works through a different publisher.

Leave it to Beethoven! This ought to get the attention of the publishers!
Publishers have always been full of trickery, but this should keep them more honest.
Beethoven has stood up for the rights and honor of composers. That's really admirable.

He was the one who named his own price for his compositions. He has done what all musicians needed to have done.

In the summer of 1802, Ludwig took his doctor's advice and went to Heiligenstadt on the outskirts of Vienna to spend some time recuperating.
Ahh, fresh air and green fields. Staying in a place like this, in and of itself, can probably cure many a serious illness.

Unfortunately, his ear pain continued to worsen, contrary to expectations. Ludwig, tormented by the pain and the fear of becoming deaf, gave up on life and even wrote a last will and testament.
Dear Carl,
When someone hears the sound of a flute in the distance and I cannot hear anything, when someone hears a shepherd calling his sheep and I cannot hear anything, I feel deeply embarrassed.
These things cause me to fall into despair and want to end my life. Every time that happens though, the only thing which sustains me is my music.
Carl, if I die, please ask the doctor to write about my illness so that people in this world can understand me a bit better after my passing. I wish you a freer life than I lived. God bless.
Ludwig van Beethoven

Mr. Beethoven!

Heh heh. Why are you walking so fast?
It's you, Rislo.

Do you hear the sound of the flute?
What sound?

Can you hear anything?
Well, I don't know. What sound are you talking about?

Nothing. This is a really quiet place.
Haha. It is a very quiet place indeed. I don't even see any shepherd boys around.

Mr. Beethoven is losing more and more of his hearing.

Ludwig began making his own music within a world in which sound did not exist. It was very experimental and free. The passion in his heart made up for whatever he might have lacked.

*oratorio: Religious opera music. Without acting or stage props, the synopsis of the storyline is read by a narrator.

Napoleon Bonaparte, who quelled a rebellion, stood up for the people, and delivered freedom and order to France. He is a true hero!

Finally, the piece dedicated to this hero is complete!

Three years since he received the request from General Bernardotte, in the spring of 1804, Symphony No. 3, Eroica, was complete. However on May 18, 1804, Ludwig was infuriated when he heard that Napoleon had taken the throne to become emperor.
Napoleon has become emperor? Is that true?

There was a coronation ceremony on May 18. And it was declared on May 20 that Napoleon was officially emperor.
I thought he was a contemporary hero who would put freedom and equality into practice... But he's made himself the emperor!

After rewriting the first page of the piece, the composition was named *Eroica*, meaning hero. In December 1804, it secretly premiered at one aristocrat's house. The following year, Beethoven performed the symphony himself at a public concert in Vienna.

The Eroica Symphony is a piece that expresses through music the image that people imagine of a true hero.
Beethoven's new symphony is finally being performed!
I wonder what it will be like.
What? It's completely different from the standard symphony.
There is no consideration for the audience!
There's no consistency and it's so loud!
This is the longest, most complicated symphony I have ever heard!
It is too difficult to understand for people like us.
The reviews from not only the audience but also the critics for Ludwig's Eroica were not very good. However, in later years, Wagner and other musicians considered the content and form of this symphony revolutionary, and Ludwig's position as a composer became well-established.

On October, 1805, France overpowered the Austrian army and occupied Vienna, which then became flooded with French soldiers.

Some time later, the first performance of Ludwig's only opera, Leonore, was held at the Theater an der Wien. The opera was about a heroic woman who sacrificed herself in order to save her husband, who had been imprisoned by a dictator.

I don't understand the content at all!

If they're thinking of performing this again, they had better change all of the songs!

This is the most boring opera I've ever seen.

In 1806, Ludwig presented *Fidelio*. It was well-received by the upper class audience but reviews from famous music critics were still not good.

After the long period Ludwig had spent working on the opera, he wrote a piece for a Russian envoy named Razumowski who was also one of his sponsors. In addition to this, he completed several other pieces.

Nevertheless, after the performance of *Fidelio*, Ludwig had no more performances at the Theater an der Wien and a rift in his relationship with his best supporter, Prince Lichnowsky, developed.

The Great Musician

CD2 Track 18 ▶

After his relationship with his best supporter, Prince Lichnowsky, went sour and his financial situation grew worse, Ludwig wrote a letter in 1807 to the Imperial Court Theater requesting aid. But they did not accept his request.

After getting surgery on an infection from a festering boil on his finger, Ludwig became busy composing his fifth and sixth symphonies and performing in concerts.
Nature never deceives me. I am so content and happy to be in the woods like this.
On December 22, 1808, he premiered the Fate Symphony, which expressed his own fate, and the Pastoral Symphony at the Theater an der Wien.
The Fate Symphony which has taken an unbelievable 13 years to complete! No, my fate will not end here. I have been born again for the sake of music!
But due to a combination of several unfortunate events, including discord within the orchestra and stage fright among the singers, Ludwig's show was a major failure.
This is so long.
I'm so sleepy I can't pay attention anymore.
The orchestra and the piano don't seem to playing together.
My, this is terrible.

After the failure of that night's performance, things became more difficult for Ludwig, and he moved into the house of one of his supporters. In 1809, he felt repulsed by life in Vienna and thought once again of leaving the city.

At this time, Napoleon's youngest brother and king of Westphalia, Jerome Bonaparte, offered him a job as a concert master, so Ludwig decided to leave Vienna.

That's not true.
We will solve your worries for you.
We cannot let Napoleon's people take Beethoven away from us.

We will provide you with a lifetime of salary so that there is no hindrance to your genius.
What can we do so that you won't leave?
Ludwig, let's not talk about leaving Vienna anymore.

If this works out, I can even get married and settle down.
Ah, the life that I so wanted to live has finally arrived!

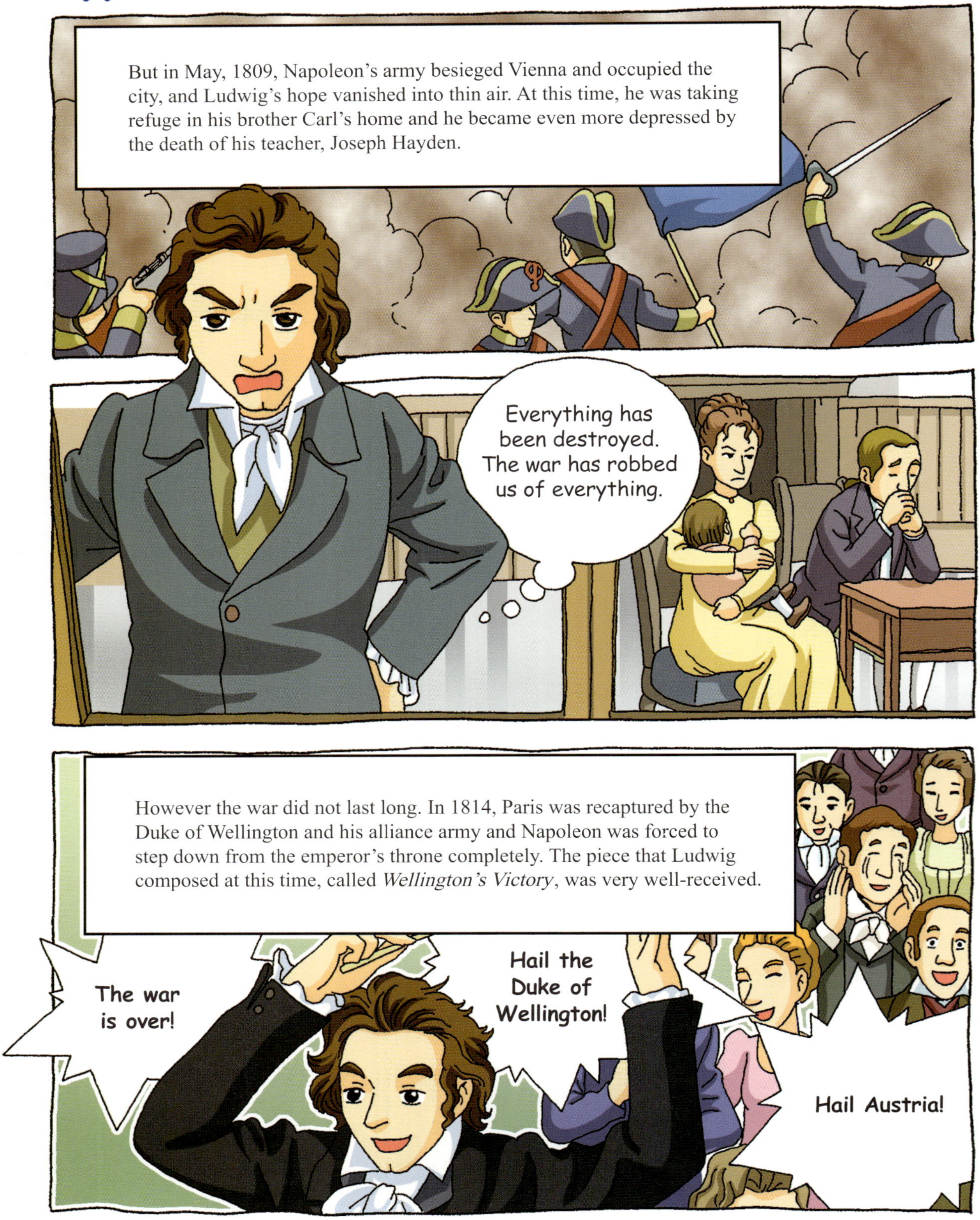

But in May, 1809, Napoleon's army besieged Vienna and occupied the city, and Ludwig's hope vanished into thin air. At this time, he was taking refuge in his brother Carl's home and he became even more depressed by the death of his teacher, Joseph Hayden.

However the war did not last long. In 1814, Paris was recaptured by the Duke of Wellington and his alliance army and Napoleon was forced to step down from the emperor's throne completely. The piece that Ludwig composed at this time, called *Wellington's Victory*, was very well-received.

Napoleon was exiled and European rulers gathered in Vienna to make a peace treaty.
This is so much fun to be able to go to a concert almost every night.
We have to commemorate for a long time the fact that peace has been reestablished.
On January 25, 1815, Ludwig was requested to play for the Russian empress. This concert would be his last as a pianist.
Pianissimo, very delicately.
Forte! Strong!
Oh my! He played the pianissimo part so lightly we couldn't even hear the notes!
Goodness! The forte part was so forceful that the piano strings are rattling!

Ludwig reached the end of his career as a pianist, hardly able to hear anything. The insecurity and sense of defeat he felt as a result threatened his creativity.
Where is the Beethoven who used to play with such inspiration?
Beethoven's not what he used to be.
He's just a pitiable handicap now.
What happened to the elaborate techniques he had?
During this difficult period, his brother, Carl, died of illness and requested that his brother look after his son. Ludwig entered into a long custody battle with Carl's wife, Johanna.
I must take care of this boy in place of my brother.
Mommy...
You will be living with me now.
I am this boy's mother!
You don't have the qualifications to be a mother. I am his guardian according to my brother's will.
This child is a gift from God to help ease my loneliness. My only child! I am going to raise him as my heir!
I want to live with Mommy!
Karl!

Ludwig, who could hardly hear anymore, began to use a hearing aid or a conversation log to converse with people starting in 1818. The court battle concerning Karl's welfare continued until 1820, five years after it began, when Ludwig finally won the case.
Now all we have to do is find a school for you.
Yes, sir.

While Ludwig was obsessed with gaining custody of his nephew, rumor spread around Vienna about his suspicious nature and unpleasant manners. In the process, many friends left him and he became a loner. Furthermore, because of the tremendous expense of Karl's education every year, Beethoven had to live a life of poverty.

Look, is anyone out there?

My jaundice is getting worse. I need to go see a doctor.

Look here, you! Stop!
Is he talking to me?

Homeless people cannot be wandering the streets like this!
What is he saying? I can't hear anything.

I'm Ludwig van Beethoven. I cannot hear, so could you write down what you're saying?
If you're Beethoven, I'm Mozart.
Let's go to the police station and take care of this.

Is that you, Mr. Beethoven?
Ah, Director!
Is he really Ludwig van Beethoven?

Yes, this is Ludwig van Beethoven.
Please release him.
We apologize for not recognizing you,
Mr. Beethoven. Your appearance...

I can understand why they mistook me for a homeless man with these clothes.
I heard Mr. Beethoven was in a very tight financial situation, but I didn't know to what extent...

In the midst of his financial difficulties and his ailing health, Ludwig continued to work hard composing music. In 1823, he completed *Missa Solemnis*. Because of his unpaid debts and constant conflicts with publishing companies, Ludwig, announced his nephew Karl as his legal heir.
It's finally finished. This work has taken four years and it's finally done.

After I die, I am going to leave all of my property to my loving nephew, Karl.
Alright. But it seems your ears are getting worse.

I know. I've got to write the symphony that the Philharmonic Society of London requested, but the pain in my ears is so bothersome.
You had better take better care of yourself.

I don't have room to think of anything else. I'm putting all I have into composing. That's the force that keeps me going.
It's nice to have an assistant who takes care of me.
That's my job as your assistant. You must be healthy in order to be able to write music, right? So please don't skip any meals.

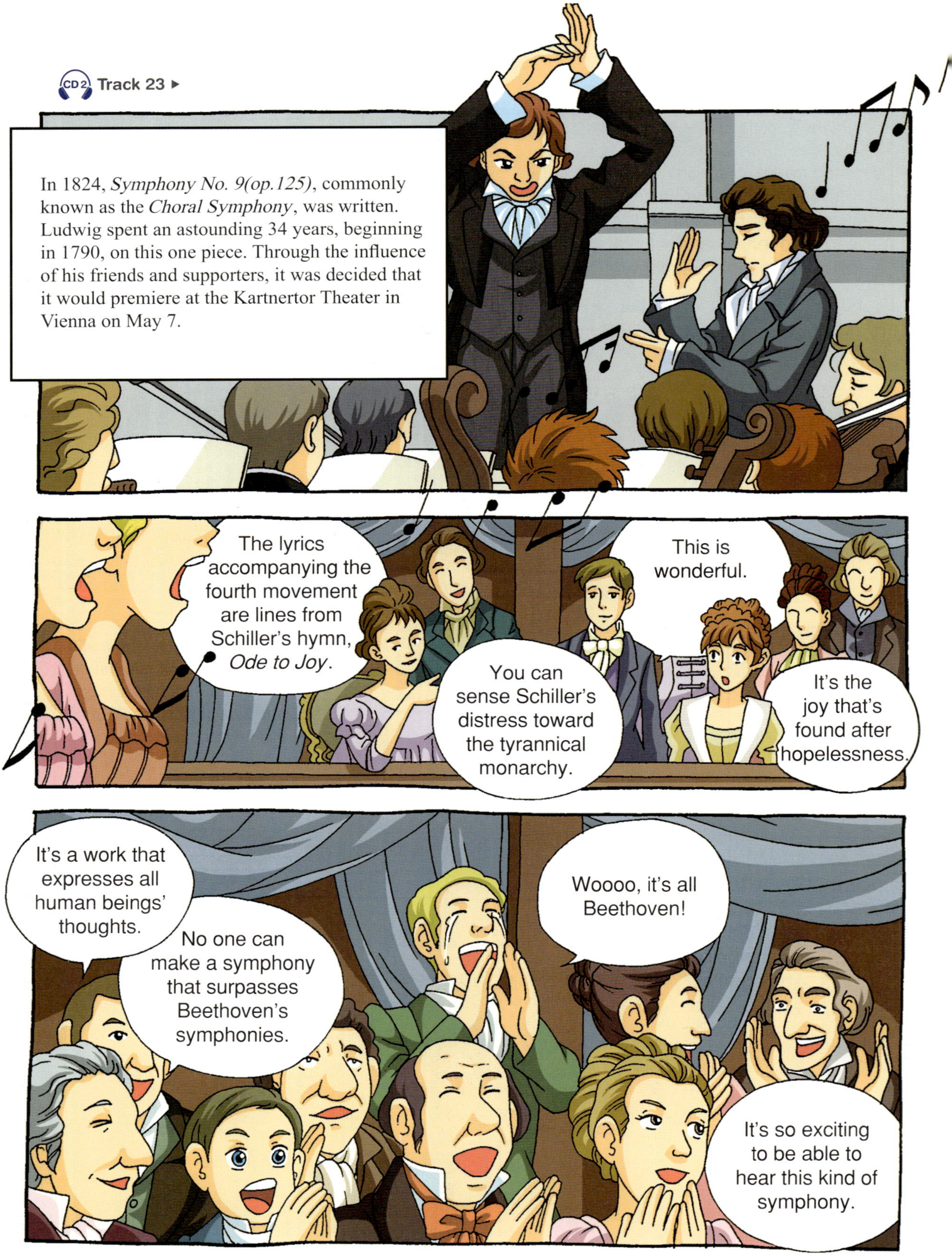

In 1824, *Symphony No. 9(op.125)*, commonly known as the *Choral Symphony*, was written. Ludwig spent an astounding 34 years, beginning in 1790, on this one piece. Through the influence of his friends and supporters, it was decided that it would premiere at the Kartnertor Theater in Vienna on May 7.

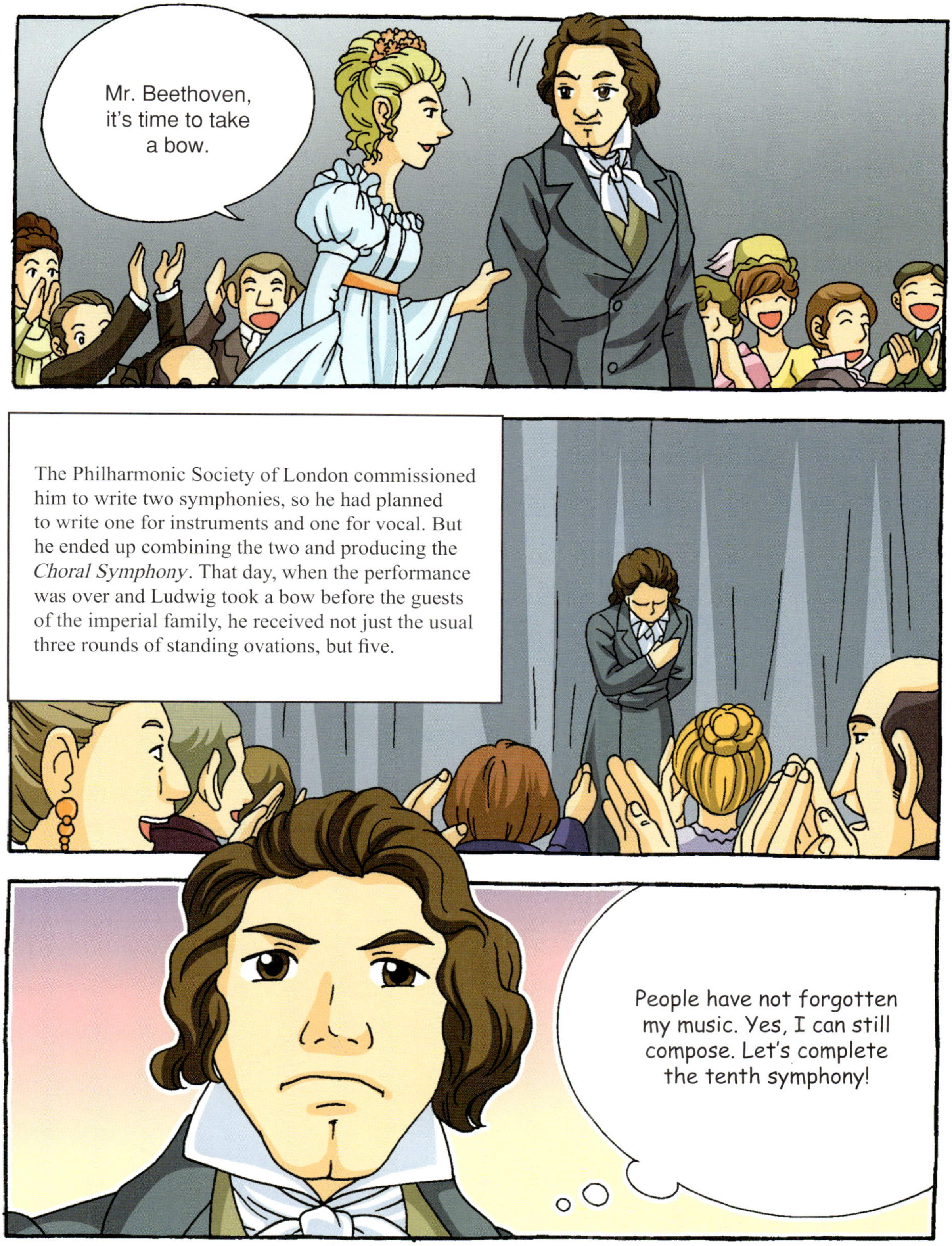

The Philharmonic Society of London commissioned him to write two symphonies, so he had planned to write one for instruments and one for vocal. But he ended up combining the two and producing the *Choral Symphony*. That day, when the performance was over and Ludwig took a bow before the guests of the imperial family, he received not just the usual three rounds of standing ovations, but five.

Karl!
The army?

You haven't even finished university and you want to enlist in the army?
I don't think studying in university is for me. Instead of studying philosophy, I would rather enlist.

You cannot. Does it make any sense to go to the army during the prime of your studying years?
If not the army, then let me go to a commercial trade school.

Well, if that's really what you want, then go ahead. But you must not meet with your mother secretly.
Yes, sir.

In 1825, Karl entered commercial trade school and Ludwig 's health worsened, causing him to spend many of his days in bed.
Mr. Beethoven! Sir!

What is it?
The police have called concerning your nephew!

Karl attempted suicide? He is not the kind of boy who would do that.
He attempted to kill himself with a pistol. When we asked him the reason...

He said that you put so much pressure on him that he wanted to die.

I did the unthinkable. You are my only child.
It's because I thought of you as my heir, who would continue my music...
To you, my fatherly embrace was a prison.
Leave me alone!
Was it so horrible that you wanted to kill yourself, Karl? I am sorry. It is all my fault.

If you're all finished packing, let's check out of the hospital.
Yes, sir.

I've decided that we're going to stay at your uncle's place in Gneixendorf for some rest.

Ludwig decided that after Karl's discharge from the hospital, he would send him to the army, as he had wished.
After spending some time there, you may go and enlist in the army.
Uncle Ludwig!

I wanted to be a good father to you, but I don't think I was successful. I want you to know that you are the most precious person to me.

After moving to Gneixendorf, Ludwig's health grew worse, making it difficult for him to keep his manners.
My eyes hurt and my stomach feels like it will burst. Please do something!

You need to refrain from wine and coffee, Mr. Beethoven.
Those are my sole pleasures! How can I refrain from them?

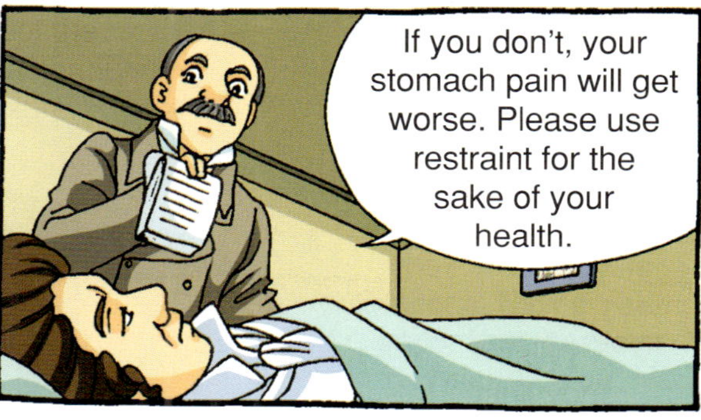

If you don't, your stomach pain will get worse. Please use restraint for the sake of your health.

How can I have a meal without any wine?

But...
I have no appetite and all I'm eating are boiled eggs. How can I not have any wine? I can't do that!

In order to continue making music, he rented a piano in 1825 and placed a large board on the strings of the piano so that he could feel the vibration of the notes.

And on the morning of December 1, 1826, Ludwig left Gneixendorf for Vienna. But en route to Vienna, he became very ill. As soon as he arrived home, he had to call for a doctor.

Well, the jaundice is quite serious and your liver has hardened. Judging from the way your stomach is bloated, it appears that your abdominal cavity is full.

The fluid needs to be removed.

On January 2, 1827, his nephew Karl left to enter the army. The next day, Ludwig wrote him a letter saying that he would bequeath all of his property to him.

The excess fluid was drained and Ludwig, whose health had improved, showed a desire to continue composing his Tenth Symphony.

I feel much better. I had better start working on the tenth symphony.

A letter for you, sir.

It's a letter from Wegeler!

Haha! He's the same as ever! Once I fully recover, I want to go on a journey with my friends.

I won't despair or give up. Once my body recovers, I've got to start composing again.

I haven't finished Symphony No. 10 yet...

But on February 27, after the fourth procedure of draining the excess fluid, Ludwig gave up all hope.

I have no more hope. My life is now over.

Don't give up.

On March 24, the wine laced with medicine was presented to Ludwig, but he could not drink it.

Pity, pity, too late.

On March 26, 1827, Ludwig, the musician who was called classical music's "holy one," breathed his last breath at about 5:45 p.m. that day. At his funeral on March 29, 1827, a crowd of 20,000 people came to mourn the death of a musical hero, including fellow musicians such as Franz Schubert and Carl Czerny, who carried his coffin.
Obey! Obey your destiny! Even if you must sacrifice, even if you become a slave...
Life is short, but music is forever.
-Taken from Beethoven's conversation Book

Lesson 1

Word Search

- Find the words which are hidden horizontally, vertically and diagonally.

S	M	Z	G	Q	M	Z	G	Q	M	Z	G	Q	J	M	Z	G	Q	P	X
W	O	V	E	R	T	U	R	E	O	N	H	W	I	N	A	H	C	I	O
E	B	M	J	A	B	Q	J	E	T	Q	A	R	B	A	R	I	O	A	M
R	Q	C	P	R	D	C	K	R	V	E	K	G	R	V	C	K	M	N	F
E	C	U	O	A	S	E	N	T	C	A	L	T	T	C	D	U	K	I	E
V	X	E	A	Y	N	P	O	Y	X	R	Q	Y	Y	X	E	N	O	S	M
E	Z	V	W	R	D	I	O	R	A	T	O	R	I	O	V	J	N	S	W
A	N	A	E	I	T	E	O	I	A	E	Z	E	S	A	R	A	E	I	I
L	S	I	R	O	S	E	C	N	S	T	R	H	O	C	G	S	R	M	T
G	D	C	U	P	D	H	T	O	D	I	E	O	P	O	H	T	B	O	P
I	M	P	R	O	V	I	S	A	T	I	O	N	M	U	U	Y	I	F	L
S	G	S	U	S	T	I	N	C	R	A	G	E	I	N	G	U	T	G	A
T	H	S	I	D	H	M	I	D	H	L	I	R	D	T	O	I	Y	H	U
O	J	A	B	S	O	R	A	F	J	T	J	A	F	E	T	J	F	J	S
C	R	E	S	C	E	N	D	O	T	I	O	N	A	R	E	B	G	K	X
H	L	A	N	H	L	E	N	R	E	E	N	H	H	P	E	N	H	L	B
J	Q	T	M	J	Q	T	A	T	T	D	O	R	I	O	Y	M	J	B	L
L	W	E	Q	L	W	Y	Q	E	W	Y	Q	L	N	I	Y	Q	L	U	E
Z	A	R	E	H	E	N	T	Z	B	K	F	Z	M	N	U	F	T	J	R
X	E	M	J	X	M	R	I	N	C	P	O	B	T	T	R	E	X	N	M
W	R	Q	F	C	R	Q	C	P	R	O	P	H	X	R	Q	C	V	R	P

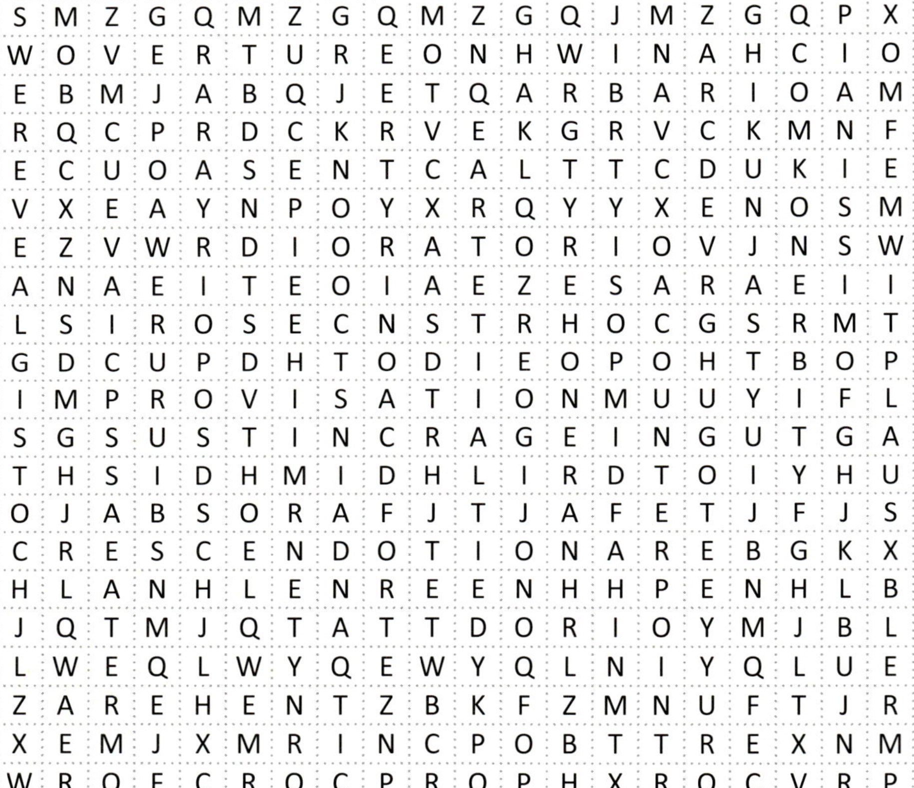

crescendo	overture	quartet	oratorio
counterpoint	improvisation	pianissimo	forte

Vocabulary

● Match each word to the correct meaning.

1. prodigy	• 협주곡
2. recital	• 거장
3. perform	• 천재, 신동
4. concerto	• 작곡하다
5. note	• 청중
6. chord	• 독주회
7. compose	• 남의 마음을 사로잡는
8. master	• 연주하다
9. maestro	• 음조, 음색
10. captivating	• 대작곡가, 명지휘자
11. symphony	• 교향곡
12. audience	• 화음, 코드

Guess What?

- Guess what he said in the blank.

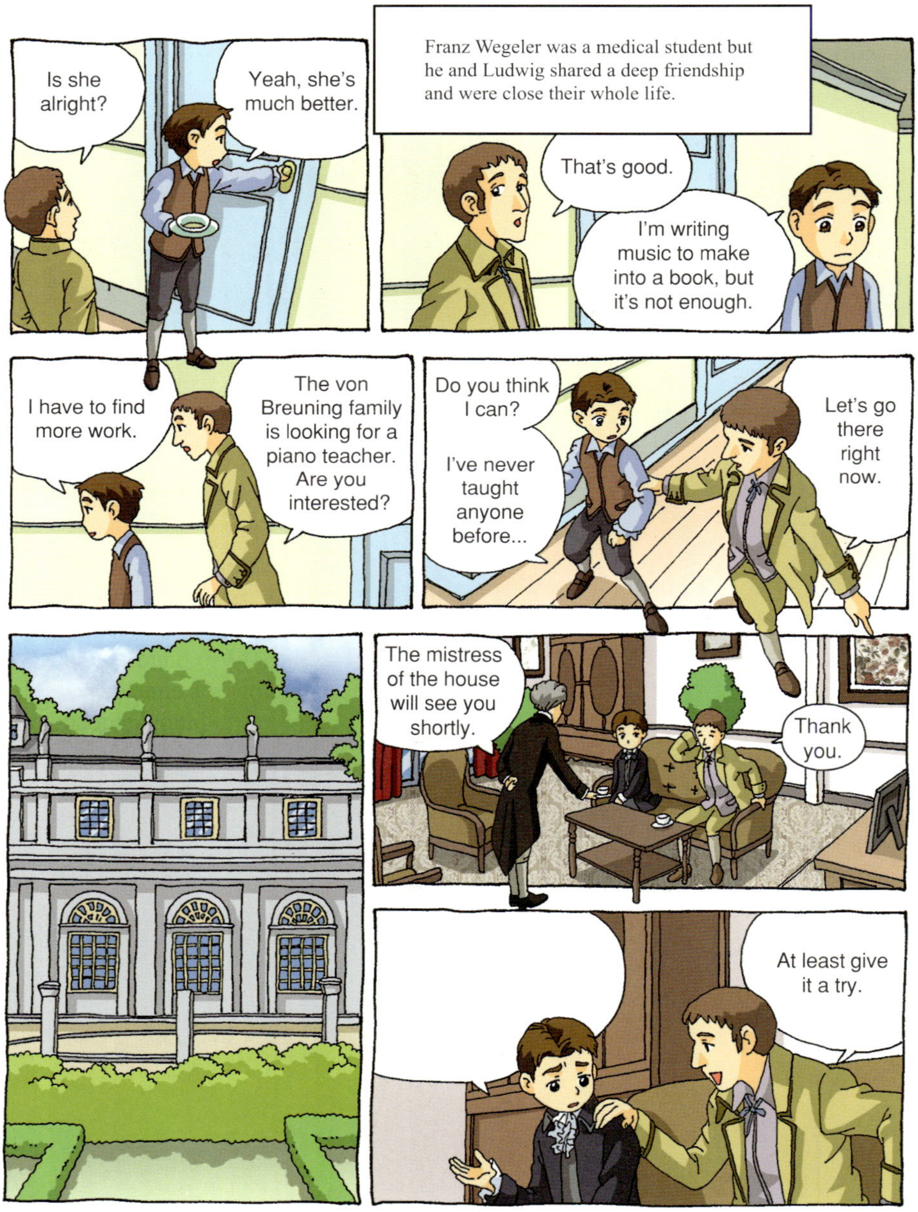

4 Meet the Orchestra

What instruments are in an orchestra? Identify the instruments that you know in the picture below and write down their names.

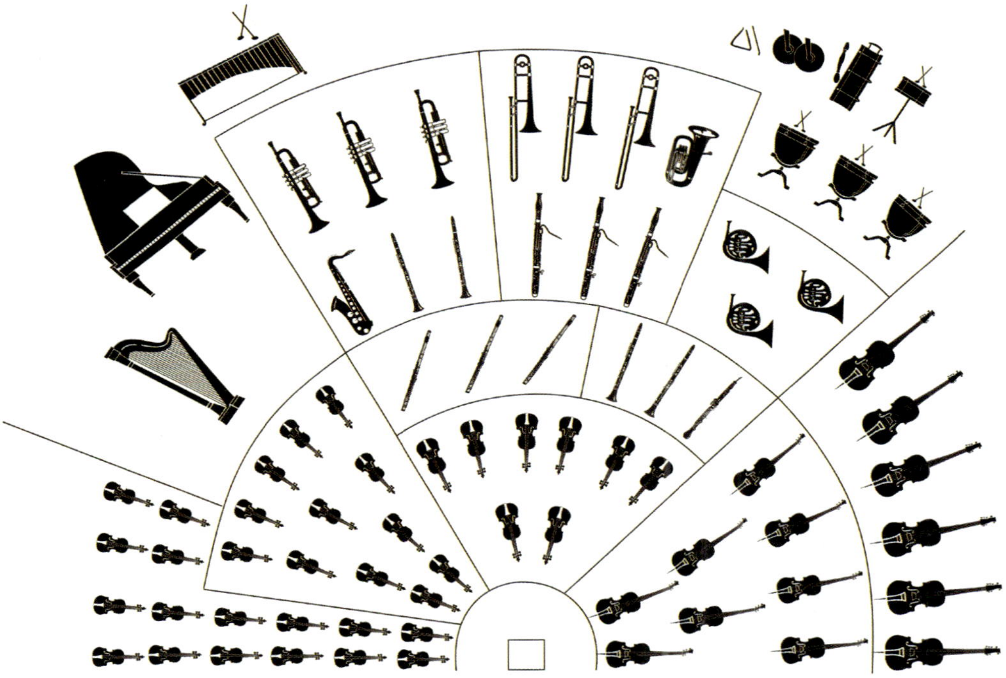

_______ piano _______   _________________   _________________

_______ harp _______   _________________   _________________

_________________   _________________   _________________

_________________   _________________   _________________

_________________   _________________   _________________

Lesson 5

Musical Instruments

Strings 현악기

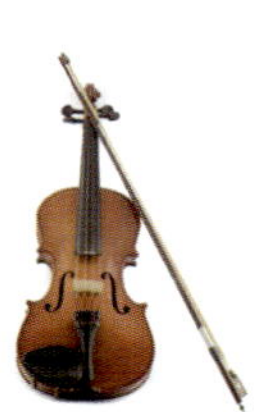

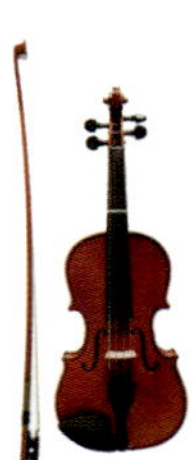

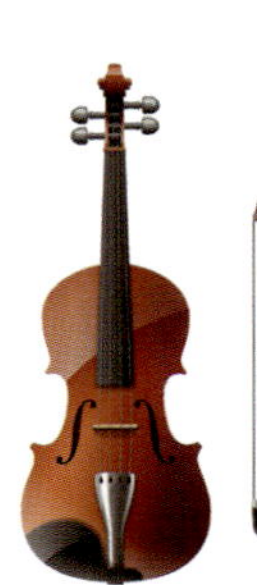

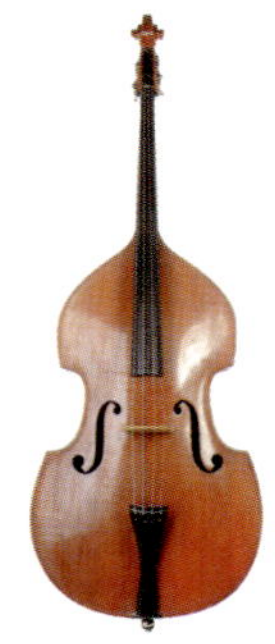

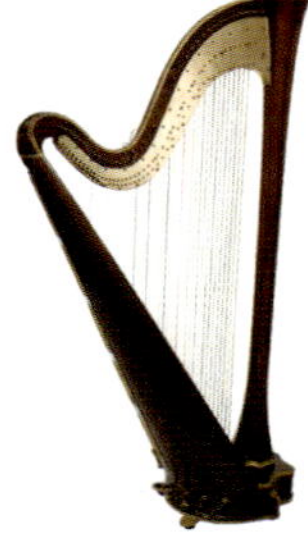

violin
바이올린

viola
비올라

cello
첼로

double bass/
contrabass
콘트라베이스

harp
하프

Woodwinds 목관악기

flute 플루트

oboe 오보에

saxophone 색소폰

piccolo 피콜로

clarinet 클라리넷

bassoon 바순

Keyboards 건반악기

pipe organ 파이프 오르간

harpsichord 하프시코드

piano 피아노

Brass 금관악기

trumpet
트럼펫

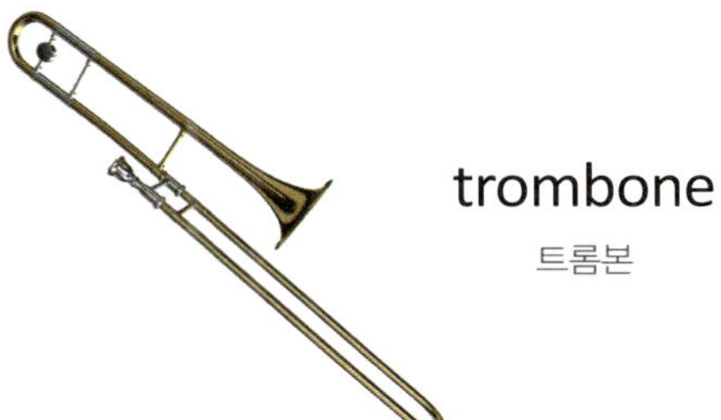

trombone
트롬본

horn/French horn
호른

tuba 튜바

Percussion 타악기

timpani 팀파니

bass drum 큰북

maracas 마라카스

tubular bells 튜블라 벨

castanets 캐스터네츠

vibraphone 비브라폰

snare drum 작은북

gong 징

triangle 트라이앵글

cymbals 심벌즈

tambourine 탬버린

xylophone 실로폰

1770년		12월 17일, 독일의 본에서 태어납니다.
1777년	7세	초등학교에 입학합니다.
1778년	8세	쾰른에서 첫 연주회를 엽니다. 이덴에게 오르간을 배웁니다.
1780년	10세	크리스찬 고트로프 네페에게 교습을 받기 시작합니다.
1781년	11세	학교를 그만두고 음악에 몰두합니다.
1783년	13세	쳄발로 주자가 됩니다. 네페가 제2의 모차르트가 될 것이라고 합니다.
1787년	17세	어머니가 세상을 떠납니다. 빈 여행에서 모차르트를 만납니다.
1792년	22세	하이든에게 가르침을 받기 위해 빈으로 유학 갑니다. 아버지가 세상을 떠납니다.
1794년	24세	알브레히츠 베르거에게 대위법, 살리에리에게 성악 작곡법을 배웁니다.
1795년	25세	〈세 개의 피아노 3중주 op. 1〉을 출간합니다.
1799년	29세	피아니스트로서 큰 성공을 거듭니다.
1801년	31세	귓병에 대해 처음으로 편지에 씁니다.

who? 01	Barack Obama	979-11-5639-023-7
who? 02	Charles Darwin	979-11-5639-024-4
who? 03	Bill Gates	979-11-5639-025-1
who? 04	Hillary Clinton	979-11-5639-026-8
who? 05	Stephen Hawking	979-11-5639-027-5
who? 06	Oprah Winfrey	979-11-5639-028-2
who? 07	Steven Spielberg	979-11-5639-029-9
who? 08	Thomas Edison	979-11-5639-030-5
who? 09	Abraham Lincoln	979-11-5639-031-2
who? 10	Martin Luther King, Jr.	979-11-5639-032-9
who? 11	Louis Braille	979-11-5639-033-6
who? 12	Albert Einstein	979-11-5639-034-3
who? 13	Jane Goodall	979-11-5639-035-0
who? 14	Walt Disney	979-11-5639-036-7
who? 15	Winston Churchill	979-11-5639-037-4
who? 16	Warren Buffett	979-11-5639-008-4
who? 17	Nelson Mandela	979-11-5639-009-1
who? 18	Steve Jobs	979-11-5639-010-7
who? 19	J. K. Rowling	979-11-5639-011-4
who? 20	Jean-Henri Fabre	979-11-5639-012-1
who? 21	Vincent van Gogh	979-11-5639-013-8
who? 22	Marie Curie	979-11-5639-014-5
who? 23	Henry David Thoreau	979-11-5639-015-2
who? 24	Andrew Carnegie	979-11-5639-016-9
who? 25	Coco Chanel	979-11-5639-017-6
who? 26	Charlie Chaplin	979-11-5639-018-3
who? 27	Ho Chi Minh	979-11-5639-019-0
who? 28	Ludwig van Beethoven	979-11-5639-020-6
who? 29	Mao Zedong	979-11-5639-021-3
who? 30	Kim Dae-jung	979-11-5639-022-0